To Michael

104 IN THE SHADE
Travels Of A Humanitarian Film Maker

*I hope you enjoy this
book as much as I enjoy
yours!
All the best*

MATTHEW ROBINSON
Muhammad Abdul Mateen

24

authorHOUSE

22. 01. 24

AuthorHouse™ UK
1663 Liberty Drive
Bloomington, IN 47403 USA
www.authorhouse.co.uk
Phone: UK TFN: 0800 0148641 (Toll Free inside the UK)
*   UK Local: (02) 0369 56322 (+44 20 3695 6322 from outside the UK)*

Published by AuthorHouse 08/09/2023

ISBN: 979-8-8230-8318-8 (sc)
ISBN: 979-8-8230-8317-1 (e)

Contents

Acknowledgements

Bismillah hir Rahman nir Rahim. In the name of God, the Most Gracious, the Most Merciful.

I give thanks to Him above all for His guidance and for the life He gives me. I thank my parents Patricia and Barry for supporting me and always being there for me, especially through my darkest times, and my brother Nicholas for being someone to look up to growing up, and throughout my life. Thank you to my children Sofia, Zain, Raeef and Ibrahim for teaching me what unconditional love is, and to better myself every day. To their mother Shaila and her family for bringing me to Islam. My step children Zayn, Hamza and Maryam for accepting me and all my idiosyncrasies. I thank the person who has given me the stability, love, patience and space to write this book, and the late nights spent reading through and editing on the fly, my eager, rudimental first/second/third/fourth/fifth drafts; my wonderful wife, soul mate and best friend, Farah.

Thank you to everyone who I have mentioned in this book. There are so many people that have been a part of my journey, that I can't mention everyone. Please know that if you have crossed paths with me, or we have worked together somewhere in the world, I thank you. I thank the people who have given me the opportunity to help them, the many communities that I have had the privilege to serve and everyone who has joined me on this journey. Thank you Steeve from Kingston Mosque, who set me on this incredible path, and whom I hold with such fondness and esteem Alhamdulillah. To Khuram who never gave up on me. I thank Irfan Rajput for his friendship and brotherhood, and for teaching me so many lessons in life and in the Humanitarian field. I thank Maroof Pirzada from Muslim Charity, who has trusted me to film in a multitude of situations around the world, and demonstrated to me, in my opinion, how every charity should operate. My Khatun 'Sistas with Blistas', who are the sisters I never had; you inspire me and make me laugh so much. I thank my friends who support me in so many different ways, I value you all.

Thank you to Michelle Akgul for proof reading, and to Joudie Kalla, Riaz Khan and Jordan Wylie MBE for taking the time to read this book and write a quote for the back cover; Immense coming from such authors, adventurers and legends as yourselves! Thank you to my dear friend and brother Dr William Barylo for writing a beautiful foreword, and giving me such valuable feedback on this book at the most critical point, that you helped give it another dimension.

Finally thank you to you, the reader, for wanting to join me on this incredible journey.

Foreword

Matt belongs to two different worlds. A world where he is Matt, the light entertainment editor for the Great British media, stuck in an opaque 'work-hard-play-hard' culture, mostly taking place in rooms as dark as his editing suite, where money flows as much as other things not worth mentioning. Then, there is another world where he is also known as Muhammad Abdul Mateen, travelling long distances to meet people affected by the worst calamities on Earth. And he's seen enough from both sides to pick which would be the direction of his life.

Such emotionally charged travels change people. I am fascinated by these stories of change. My own life has been one of travels, witnessing human distress and adopting a faith which was not my parents'; and this is perhaps why Matt's journey resonates with me. It offers a glimpse of what someone has to go through when undertaking humanitarian work; and how, as humans, when thrown into contexts where we can't decipher people's speech, we universally understand each others' language of emotions.

I am very lucky to know the Matt from behind the scenes and to have had a glimpse of the many challenges he has overcome – what you will find in the book is just the surface. These experiences don't leave the mind to rest; they lead us to question our very purpose on Earth. These are the reflections Matt shares through this journey to self-realisation. The various situations he has been put through, the scares, the horror, the relief, and the joy through the varied human experiences he shared, and how all of these made him who he is today.

For many who enjoy a certain level of comfort, such a leap between two worlds can appear too scary to be reasonable. Why, like Matt, would one trade the comfort of an editing suite for a life of sweat, tears and mosquito stings – all that with a pay cut and the instability of temporary contracts? Perhaps, like Matt, we all have a calling that modern society and work culture push us to suppress for the sake of proving our worth to people who judge us by the figures in our bank accounts. How did Matt do it? This unfolds in the pages that are to follow.

The charity sector too, has its darker side: humanitarian work has become for many a status symbol, a branding or marketing ploy at the expense of the aid provided to people suffering. While Matt has had a glimpse of it, the book rather focuses on the concrete and personal experiences he had on the field. While he confesses how this life of travels tickles his childhood's ego and adventurer dreams, his intentions have always been to put people first – and I know this through the countless pro-bono documentaries he has produced, at home, for the causes he believes in.

Matt's journey has proven that even if one cannot always tangibly change the condition of those who suffer, one can at least relay their voices through the medium of film… and perhaps, as you will find out towards the end of the book, create their own, independent, human-scale initiative.

Enjoy this read, and allow yourself to be fully immersed in each moment.

Dr William Barylo - May 2023

Prologue

My idea of paradise was running around the fields of my grandparents, Alexander and Doris Gifford's small farm, near Bitton, just outside of Bristol. Imagining I was trekking across the Sahara desert, or mining for diamonds, gold and lost treasure. Or sniping at my big brother Nicholas through the long grass on the cusp of haymaking season. I was German, he was always the allies. I always lost of course, as that is what the history books say. Mum was a nurse and dad was a carpenter. We grew up in Wick, a village between Bath and Bristol, and they blessed us with a loving childhood. Bike rides along country lanes, night treks with the scouts, camping holidays in Devon and Cornwall... all fired an already over-zealous imagination. I used to play football for the cubs and rugby, swimming and hockey at school, and the teams I supported were Bristol Rovers football club and Bath Rugby. The Rovers has been ingrained in my family for generations on all sides, and it's an obsession that I still have today. I used to love watching movies on the TV or the VHS recorder, and my favourite film was Raiders of the Lost Ark. I suppose the person I wanted to be most like was Indiana Jones (Still do today!). I wanted to join the army to drive tanks, but never had the guts for it. When I found out I'd have to go to Northern Ireland, maybe get shot at and have to shoot at people, it rather put me off the idea.

Art was my thing, and after a couple of successes in school exhibitions; winning the John Lennon art award at sixteen; getting A* in my Art A-level at St Mary Redcliffe and Temple School in Bristol; against all expectations, I barely scraped through my art foundation course at Sydney Place, in Bath. From being the best in school, to suddenly be surrounded by other more talented artists was something I found very challenging and intimidating. The freedom of suddenly going to an art foundation course after seven years of attending a strict school was too much for me to handle, and I spent much of my time down the pub or hanging out with my mate Kerryn, a chef from Barbados. In fact, I virtually moved onto his sofa and became a part of the fixtures and fittings with his very patient and understanding wife Sonia, and their kids Donna, Philippa, Danielle, and Ezekiel for the next three years. I loved to party, and subsequently failed to get into any of the art colleges I had applied to, to study a Fine Art degree in Painting. After four years of being immersed in the rave scene of the early 1990's, a surreal four months in Tenerife selling semi precious stones and chillumns on the beach, and some absolutely soul destroying jobs, I fell into media college by accident. It was here that I encountered two things that would change my life forever; editing and Islam.

Just before I attended Bath Media college, I had read a book called Jupiters Travels, written by a journalist called Ted Simon, who had travelled around the world solo on a Triumph Tiger motorbike from 1974-1977. It was so well written and so inspiring, I read it cover to cover and then read it again. (this was the book which inspired Ewan MacGregor and Charley Boorman to do the 'Long Way Round' and 'Long Way Down'). This too was my dream. To have adventures and to travel.

I wanted to be a war correspondent or frontline cameraman, until a friend told me that her father had been one, became an alcoholic and then took his own life through the horrors he had witnessed. I was deterred by this, because as much as I wanted to see myself as an adventurer, I realised that deep down, it was something I was terrified of doing. Scared of fighting; of getting hit; of seeing trauma, death and destruction. Scared of dying. In fact I pretty much lived my life in fear of everything or so I thought, and I had very low self esteem. I was always searching for validation from anyone and anywhere, but when it really came down to it, my biggest critic and doubter was me. I had imposter syndrome with most things I did. Where this came from I still don't fully know, but I believe it started as early as primary school. The perception of not being heard, not being included and at times being alienated or laughed at. In secondary school it was down to being bullied mercilessly, which upon reflection I now put down to my undiagnosed Autism. However, I still yearned to travel and have adventures.

Punctuality also wasn't my strongest point, and when I turned up late for class yet again, (I lived opposite the college) I was made an example of and told to have a go at the editing first. I wasn't very interested, as editors, according to the stereotype of the day, were fat beardy men in Aaron jumpers, who were very rude and opinionated. This turned out to be true, but I had a go and was hooked, and it set me on a career path for the next twenty five years.

As with most educational courses, I was expected to write an essay, and being a media course, it was of an investigative nature. One of the ten essay questions we could choose from was "The Representation of Islam in The British Media'. Now this jumped off the page at me for a number of reasons. Even though I went to a Church Of England secondary school, I had never really got the concept of Jesus being God's only son, and had turned my back on organised religion at the age of 13. My mum had always said that Yasser Arafat was a good man and that what Israel was doing to the Palestinian people was wrong, unfair and inhumane. However, being telegraph readers, the broadsheets opinion was very different. Israeli 'settlers', 'civilians', and 'farmers'. Palestinian 'extremists', 'separatists', 'terrorists'.. a real disparity of language. I thought to myself, 'My mum is a good judge of character so something isn't right'. I decided to follow up on this essay question, and visited the Mosque in Bath. Shaved head, eyebrow pierced and earring, I think they thought I was there to kick off. Luckily the imam saw through that, opened the door to me and brought me into the mosque. We sat down and spoke about Islam and the Qur'an for a while. When I left, I decided that if I were to pick a religion, it would be Islam as it is logical, forward thinking, scientific, and has a loving set of guidelines to live my life by, if I needed it, which I didn't at that time. However, if I did, then Islam would be the one.

In July 2000, I moved to London to start my Film and TV editing career. As the divine plan would unfold itself, the following spring I met someone, and asked them to marry me. Being Muslim and hailing from a British Pakistani family, meant that I would need to embrace Islam. Islam? I knew all about that! No problem at all! So in July 2001, I took the 'Shahada' (declaration of faith) in the

Faisal Mosque in Islamabad, and got married. Allah blessed us with four beautiful children, Alhamdulillah, one of whom is non-verbal autistic, and needs 24 hour care.

Fifteen years down the line, most of those spent in an edit suite working on shows such as Big Brother, 2006 Fifa World Cup, The Only Way Is Essex, This Morning, Richard and Judy, X-Factor and Britain's Got Talent, I had had enough light entertainment to last me a lifetime. The never ending monotony of sitting in a dark room and staring at screens merged into one big painful and unhealthy experience. It was time for a change. My marriage was very difficult and had been negatively impacted for years, due to many factors, including my work, and it eventually disintegrated. I had been told by a doctor at the age of 40 that I had ADHD and was most probably a person living with high functioning Autism, which made a lot of my confusing life growing up make sense retrospectively. However, I was still left with myself. Not easy, I can tell you. Sometimes I was depressed or had intrusive thoughts, mainly fear based self loathing, insecurity and paranoia, due to the out of control lifestyle I was immersed in. It was a very painful place to be, and as a result, I was cut off and behind an emotional brick wall. Even though I had embraced Islam, I was still a very lost soul.

In 2014 after being a nominal Muslim for thirteen years, and not having much knowledge or practicing the religion at all, my middle son asked me to go to Kingston-Upon-Thames mosque with him, where I met Brother Salim from Martinique, also a Muslim by choice. Salim helped me learn to pray properly, and even though I was battling my own personal issues, I tried to throw myself into a more spiritual way of life. His guidance and that of others there helped me truly begin to understand more about Islam, my journey through it and my relationship with God. The things I learned from Salim were vital for the start of my practising journey. How to pray; how to dress appropriately for prayer; how to speak calmly and kindly; Islamic etiquette in the mosque, and in everyday life. Alhamdulillah! Kingston Mosque for me, was the true beginning of my journey of understanding and enlightenment through Islam. There was a good mix of people from all nationalities, including

Pakistani, Moroccan, Algerian, Libyan, Senegalese, Nigerian, Egyptian, Bangladeshi .. the list goes on. Every nation and culture have their own slightly nuanced ways of worship, but in Kingston mosque it was definitely focused on the 'Sunnah', or habits and ways of the Prophet Muhammed (Peace be Upon Him) rather than cultural leanings. This to me as a revert (convert), was hugely appealing.

I had told brother Salim of my spiritual disquiet with the work I was doing in mainstream TV and that I was looking for something more in tune with my faith. I had been working on a well known horror gameshow, and as an editor, I needed to put myself in a really dark place to think in a scary way. This really impacted my mental and emotional health, so when in 2016 Salim brought to my attention a job opportunity as a videographer for a charity based in South West London, I jumped at the chance. I took the job at Muntada Aid in June 2016. My life would never be the same again.

In this collection of my travel experiences, some of the names and identities of people have been omitted or changed, but the events, countries and timelines remain faithful to the truth.

1

Aid Convoy To Greece

'It is estimated that between 80,000 and 100,000 refugees fled to Greece between 2011 - 2016, mainly due to the war in Syria. Around 4,000 people drowned whilst making the perilous crossing from Turkey to Greece. The figure as of November 2021, of refugees travelling to Greece is more than 1 million people.'

Data source - UNHCR

In June 2016, I took a job as videographer for a charity based in West London, called Muntada Aid. I had to take a huge pay cut to do this work, but for a long time now, I had felt that the light entertainment editing I had been doing had broken me through long hours, intense schedules and the accompanying lifestyle, and a change was needed. Something that could make a tangible difference to peoples lives. Muntada was interesting on so many levels; based over at West London Islamic Cultural Centre at Parsons Green mosque, it was part of the umbrella organisation Al-Muntada Trust. The small speakers in the corner of the office would announce the call to prayer, and we would all head downstairs into the mosque and pray. There were very specific rules with the charity, and one in particular which appealed to me, was backbiting being a sackable offence. Backbiting is another word for backchatting someone negatively. It's like slander or malicious gossip and the Hadith (an authentic saying of the Prophet Muhammad peace be upon him) is as follows:

Abu Huraira reported: The Messenger of Allah, peace and blessings be upon him, said, "Do you know what backbiting is?" They said, "Allah and his messenger know best." The

1

> *Prophet said, "To mention your brother in a way he dislikes."*
> *It was said, "What do you think if what I said about him is*
> *true?" The Prophet said, "If what you say about him is true,*
> *it is backbiting. If it is not true, it is slander."*
>
> *Source: Ṣaḥīḥ Muslim 2589*

For this to be banned was something I found very proper and very refreshing.

Within a few weeks, the first foreign assignment came up. I was to fly to Greece to film the distribution of aid to Syrian, Iraqi and Kurdish refugees in the various camps in and around Thessaloniki. The aid convoy was organised and run by Hope and Aid Direct, a charity founded by Charles Storer MBE, that had been running aid convoys for a quarter of a century, since the Kosovo War back in the mid 1990's. I had been to Bristol to film the loading of the trucks, met Charles and the team and was preparing to fly out, when the idea hit me to follow the convoy, overland on its five-day journey across Europe, filming and uploading daily updates along the route. We had to be quick as it was a last minute change of plan, but we sorted the logistics, flights were cancelled and a car was booked. (It only had 16 miles on the clock when we hired it, and over 3000 when it was returned). Suddenly this was all becoming very real.

Only weeks before I had been sat in an edit suite staring at film of wild animals and sea birds in Cape Town, South Africa, and now I was about to set off on a real adventure. We packed our bags, went through our check list and were ready for the epic road trip ahead. Kabir Miah, a humanitarian lawyer who moved into the charity sector a decade ago, was the program officer for this aid convoy, and we were going to be spending the next five days, seven countries and 1834 miles sat next to each other.

We set off early one Sunday morning in July and met up with Charles and the other drivers at the east bound services on the M2. I had my trusty Canon EOS 7D and Tamron 18-55mm f2.8 lens, and started filming. There were 3 trucks in total; one articulated lorry and trailer called 'Solent Challenger' and two 7.5 ton trucks called 'Frantic' and 'Robin Hood'; all laden with clothes, toiletries, tinned food, cleaning products, and shoes amongst many other items. We met with the two 7.5 ton trucks, and were to meet the big rig somewhere in Germany as it had set off a couple of days beforehand. Charles set our car up with a CB (citizens band) radio and very long antennae stuck to the roof with a strong magnet base, and our CB handle for any communication along the route was 'Matt-Kab', as in Matt and Kabir, just a shortened conjoined version, easier to shout down the radio if need be. As the convoy pulled out of the services and on to the M2, another wave of excitement hit me, but also tinged with apprehension and nerves. That ever present imposter syndrome started to raise its ugly head.. 'Am I really up to this? Will I be able to handle the situation? Will I let myself and everyone else down?' I quietened the voices of doubt in my mind and focused on the road ahead. We were on our way to Greece, and the next five days were definitely going to be a test of character, whatever adventures, pitfalls and perils lay ahead.

In a few hours we had crossed the channel, and were driving through the lowlands of France, Belgium and arriving at Aachen in Germany just after the sun had set. Aachen is a medieval town on the Belgium-Germany border. There is a castle and an old town, where we stayed in a quaint hotel for our first night. I can't remember its name, but I do remember being very hungry after such a long drive, and taking in some Turkish kebab, and going for a stroll through the old town by Aachen Cathedral.

At seven early the next morning, we were back on the road and had caught up with the convoy just outside Frankfurt. We pulled into a service station and Charles had already fired up the burner in the back of his truck and was serving his legendary hearty fry up breakfast to the drivers. There was Charles' co-driver Anthony, a BT manager from Ireland driving Robin hood, and Bill and Cynthia in their 70's who were driving 'Frantic'. I interviewed Charles about Hope And Aid Direct, the ethos of what they do and of his experiences on the road and in the numerous refugee camps he had been to. After the interview, Charles asked me if I had ever been to a refugee camp, to which I replied 'no'. His response was 'It will change your life forever'. I understood his words and took them on board, but really had no true understanding of what he meant. But he was right, as I was to discover only a few days later.

After a long hot drive through Bavaria, past Würzburg through rolling hills, forests and giant wind turbines, which rose up from the landscape in pretty much every direction, we arrived at a services near Beyerischer Wald. It was here that we finally met up with the big rig 'Solent Challenger' and its driver Roddy from Scotland, who had set off a day before with his co-driver Bernie, and was glad to see us. We all sat down outside and ate dinner together for the first time on this trip, talking about anything and everything; a real sense of camaraderie already. The jokes were flowing and everyone was at ease. We had covered just over 700 miles in two solid days and were already starting to feel tired. The drivers turned in for the night in their truck cab beds and Kabir and I headed off into the hot humid Bavarian night to try to find the guest house we had booked somewhere in the hills near the service station. The Satnav took us down some windy narrow lanes until it showed us we had arrived at Bogenberg Gasthof 'Zur schönen Aussicht', or 'The Beautiful View'. We finally pulled up outside the quaint single story Gasthof (Guest house), surrounded by trees on a hillside. Crickets were chirping, the night was close and the air was full of mosquitos. A short lady came out to greet us and by this time it was pitched black, and the whole scene resembled something from a Dracula movie. Our host was very warm and welcoming, invited us in and brought us a refreshing lemonade. The view from the wooden garden veranda was indeed incredible. The full moon made the Danube river shine like a meandering ribbon through the valley floor. It was such a beautiful and peaceful place to be, apart from the swarms of midges and mosquitos. They won in the end and we retired to our rooms.

This was our first problem day. We had all crossed over the border into Austria and were passing Linz when the Articulated lorry had a tyre blow out. Kabir pulled up on the hard shoulder in front of the trucks and we walked back, only to see two pairs of legs sticking out from underneath the cab. Charles and Roddy were surveying the damage and a replacement tyre was needed. A very kind garage nearby changed the tyre over with the spare for free, but we still needed to find a replacement tyre. There were still over 1000 miles to go with the desperately needed cargo and the roads weren't going to be getting any better. Using the time tested resource of social media, I posted on Facebook about the blow out and within an hour had a response from a Lajos, a Hungarian friend and fellow editor, living in London. He said he could source the tyre in Budapest and as we were to be crossing over the border into Hungary in 150 miles or so, it seemed like there was a divine plan in action. After crossing the border into Hungary and heading toward Budapest, we arrived at the tyre place in what seemed like a derelict soviet era trading estate. Everything was rusted, broken glass and high weeds everywhere; like an industrial scene from a film by Russian director Sergei Bodrov. Sadly the tyre was the wrong size and was partially worn, which was no good and frustrated everyone even more. However, Lajos's second option came through and we arranged to collect the tyre the following morning. The trucks all headed out of the city to park up for the night at motorway services whilst Kabir and I headed into Budapest. We stayed in a lovely hotel at the top of the hill in Buda, went for halal Chinese food with some of Kabir's friends and then retired for another early night.

On the fourth morning, we found ourselves on another industrial estate on the outskirts of Budapest. Once we had collected the tyre, we had to put our foot down to catch up with the convoy, which was already crossing over the border into Romania. Apparently they had queued for four hours and the artic had been told to turn around and head for another border crossing. In the end, common sense prevailed and the Hungarian border force allowed the trucks to cross over into Romania. Kabir and I, however weren't so lucky.

As we had approached the border checkpoint, one of the Hungarian border force guards had seen me filming. That was like a red rag to a bull. They pulled us over, asked us where we had come from, where we were going, with whom, why and for how long. They made us take every item of equipment, clothing, underpants, socks, deodorant, etc., and lay them out individually on the tarmac so they could inspect them. Once they realised that they had no reason to stop us continuing on our journey, they let us pack away our kit and pass through the border. The Romanians looked at our passports and waved us through without incident, and within minutes we were driving though flat lowlands of yet another country. It all looked very plain and boring, surrounded by fields of cabbages and sunflowers, split by soviet era metal power pylons, threading through the flat and foreboding landscape like never ending washing lines. There was a pervading sense of low oppressive energy, which Kabir and I both felt, yet couldn't explain. This went on for hours, until the EU funded motorway ran out and the rutted and potholed roads of Romania greeted us. Also, there was a sudden change in scenery, which also affected the heavy mood we were experiencing. Flat fields and pylons gave way to green forests and winding roads through the hills, and our mood lifted once more. Every now and then, we would have a go at reaching the convoy on our CB radio, and finally the voice of Charles crackled through the radio, describing where the convoy was parked up and waiting for us.

I jumped in the big rig with Roddy, a quietly assured man in his sixties, and we headed along the banks of the Danube. By this point the Danube was a huge mass of water, almost a kilometre wide, moving slowly south eastwards towards the Black Sea. On the other side of the river was Serbia, and there was a long hydro electric pontoon bridge joining the two countries. The convoy pulled into the Restaurant Taverna Sârbului, just outside the town of Drobeta-Turnu Severin. Here we were served the tastiest fish dishes, with Pike, Carp and Bream amongst items on the menu.

One of my greatest pleasures on all these trips has always been to have a coffee and cigarette, wherever I am in the world. So to sit on the banks of the great Danube River, watching the gigantic mass of water flowing before me, with a cigarette, a cup of strong fresh coffee and the evening summer sun beating down on my face was a moment of bliss I shall never forget. So far so good.. no real problems as such, and we had completed three quarters of the road trip. At night I was editing in the hotel rooms and was sending the one minute films to HQ to be uploaded to social media. This made for very long days indeed, and it was starting to add pressure to the already tiring hours on the road. Anxiety and nerves started to rise once more and I had to ground myself in the moment. Just where I was right now. Once more staring into the huge mass of slowly moving water in front of me; feeling the heat of the sun on my face; tuning in to the chirp of the crickets; We were on a road trip, however not just any old trip, but an aid convoy road trip, on the way to help refugees fleeing the war in Iraq and Syria. It truly was a feeling of being alive, of being in the moment and to finally be a part of something that was making a tangible difference to other peoples lives. Alhamdulillah.

As usual, Kabir and I left the others to sleep in their trucks and we headed to another guest house. This was like something out of the 1980's. Gawdy decor, Artex patterned walls and ceilings, red faux leather vinyl chair covers and fluffy quilted blankets with roses on. But it was clean, secure, and a fine recipe for sleep. Once I had finished the edit, I soon drifted off.

The sun was just over the horizon when we jumped into the car and headed to a petrol station in town. I think that this was the one of the few times on the trip I was actually scared. There were packs of wild and stray dogs everywhere. All laid out in the morning sun, but definitely paying an interest in us foreigners filling up with fuel and snacks. As a child, I used to deliver a local church magazine, and one of the neighbours had a large German Shepherd. The dog had growled at me as I opened the gate, but the owner reassured me that he would be fine, and wouldn't bite me. Handing over the magazine, the dog jumped up and bit my arm. Ever since then, I have a fear of angry looking or feral dogs. It was also the thought of rabies that scared me, however on this trip and probably on every trip I have taken since, I don't go near the animals. Apart from Hyenas, but that's a story for another chapter.

Again I hopped into the big rig with Roddy and we trundled off through the beautiful Romanian countryside. Hills, farms, rivers, trees, herds of cattle blocking the road..a little bit like going back in time. The crossing to Bulgaria was uneventful and we were soon driving along dusty pot holed roads in what seemed like the middle of nowhere. What I did notice, was every mile or so, there was a woman sat at the side of the road. These women had been dropped off earlier that day by organised crime gangs and were sat there to sell themselves to any passing driver who wanted their services. Apparently this was very common in Bulgaria, alongside a rise in drug use and HIV. The women were picked up at the end of the day and taken back to their bosses.

Around 8pm, we arrived at the border with Greece. We had been on the road for 5 days straight and were now looking forward to being based in one place for a few days. This last leg of the drive took a few hours, but it was reassuring to finally see the word THESSALONIKI on the overhead road signs. The rear of Robin Hood truck was illuminated in our headlights as dusk enveloped us, and we followed in convoy toward the twinkling lights of the city. It was dark by the time we arrived at the outskirts of Thessaloniki and we pulled into our hotel car park. We were welcomed by the team of 'Hope And Aid Direct' volunteers who had just flown in from the UK and were eager like us, to get out to the refugee camps with the Aid. Introductions were made, a late night dinner of kebabs, rice and chicken was served, and we all fell into our beds, exhausted.

* * *

Dawn brought breakfast, a briefing, excitement and a temperature of 35ºC. Charles set out some very simple guidelines and told us what to expect from the day. We were going to a large warehouse in the town where all of the aid would be stored then sorted and distributed to camps that were in need. The drive to the warehouse wasn't long at all and in no time, we were backing the trucks up to the warehouse entrance. The forklift truck had broken down so Charles and the warehouse manager Robbie, (previously a captain in the Croatian army), were busy sourcing another one. The volunteers were given certain tasks to do, which consisted of unpacking, sorting and then making an assembly line to pack emergency boxes to be given to families in the refugee camps. Around 6pm in the evening, we received a call to go to a refugee camp on the slopes of Mount Olympus.

Petros Olympus camp was a former mental asylum, and was not the easiest place to get to. The trucks had to wind up sharp bends and narrow roads until the vast sprawling sea of tents came into view. A sharp hairpin turn into the camp, and we were met by a group of children and adults. The truck rolled down into the centre of the camp, and past a group of children playing football. I just couldn't help myself. I ran amongst them, camera slung over my shoulder and shouted 'On my head', whilst tapping my head. One of the boys teed up the semi deflated worn ball, and walloped it up into the air. A perfect arc, and right onto my sweaty bald sunburned forehead… The ball glanced off, past the outstretched goalie and into the bottom corner of the post. I burst into a goal celebration which was more of surprise than anything else (football had never been my strong game) and was surrounded by high-fiving kids. My sports crowning glory was captured on film by Rebecca Spencer, Muntada's PR officer. Rebecca had landed the day before with the volunteers and was here to take photos, write about the aid delivery and get an insight into the demographic and needs of the refugees.

It was a hot summers evening and the camp was being sprayed with insect repellent… a buzzing and crackling noise radiating in the background. The back of the truck was open and the volunteers formed a human chain, along with some of the men of the camp, and began unloading into a secure store room. Next to this was a bank of hand basins, obviously installed by UNHCR, where the children were playing, mothers washing clothes and men stood around smoking. These refugees were Yazidi. The Yazidi mainly come from Iraq, Syria, Turkey, parts of Iran and the Caucuses. The religion is an amalgamation of ancient Persian religions and elements of Judaism, Christianity and Islam. They are only permitted to marry within their own community and have faced persecution for centuries due to differing takes on what and who they worship. The main deity is Malk Ta'us, or 'Peacock Angel' and worshipped in the form of a Peacock. This has also been interpreted by some as 'Satanic' and devil worship, hence the alienation and persecution over the centuries. Their lands and homes had been taken over by

Islamic State, and for this very reason, they were being persecuted in the most obscene and horrific manner.

We spoke to a few of the camp residents. One had been there for months, had no idea of where they were heading, but wanted to aim for Germany or the UK. Another was with his family, consisting of mother, father, uncle, aunt and children. He showed me something I will never forget. It was a photo of a group of teenage Yazidi girls, all in orange boiler suits and packed into a cage. He started to break down crying when he described what had happened to them. The monsters from the so called Islamic State then doused them with petrol and burned them alive. This was not a rare occurrence apparently. Yazidi women had been taken as sex slaves too, and were beaten and abused often to death. The men that had been captured were all dead. Executed. I will never forget how I felt in that moment; a feeling of fluttering panic in my chest, catching my breath over something so incomprehensibly horrific. These refugees had been through an unimaginable hell and were existing like the living dead. On a hillside, in tents.

We returned to the truck and with a human chain, started to unload the goods. There were tinned foods, dried foods, rice, pasta, flour, sugar, personal hygiene goods, clothes and shoes. Everything was stacked into a locked store room and would be distributed to the camp inhabitants by the camp authorities when we had departed. Once the truck was unloaded, we said our goodbyes and promised to bring some new footballs on our next visit. Kind of buzzing yet stunned, I got into the car and we left the way we came. My first visit to a refugee camp. As Charles had eluded to three days earlier, my life would indeed never be the same again.

The second day started early, with a run to Softex refugee camp near the centre of Thessaloniki. The purpose of our visit was to do a recce and see what the main needs of the camp's residents were. As we arrived at the gates, we were told that we weren't allowed to go in. This was the point I realised that the quiet, mild mannered, educated and polite Kabir, was actually a lion. He demanded to see the commanding officer, a colonel in the Greek Army. I'm not sure of the exact contents of their conversation, but what I do know is that Kabir scolded him so severely and ordered to speak to his commanding officer, that the colonel submitted and said we could go in at our own risk and that we weren't their responsibility. We weren't prepared for what we were about to experience.

Softex was a disused toilet roll factory that had been set up as a short term makeshift refugee camp. People had been living here for months and the conditions were not good. As we made our way into the factory itself, a derelict building with a high ceiling, we saw row upon row of faded green tents, the roofs covered in a fine red dust. People were selling cigarettes, sweets and a few toiletries on top of upturned cardboard boxes. It was very noisy, in the sense there were a lot of people talking, shouting and children playing. I was approached by a boy no older than 10 years old; his name was Ali. He asked us to follow him to his tent, where we met his mother and younger siblings. They had fled Aleppo in Syria and had been in the camp for 2 months, after their death defying trip across the sea. His father hadn't been heard from and was presumed dead, killed in the fighting in Syria. Our translator Farah, who herself had escaped from Iraq told us that the family never get any rest, there is too much noise, high temperatures, insanitary conditions and fights regularly break out between men who are addicted to prescription drugs smuggled into the camp. Their situation felt helpless, so we gave the mother a small bundle of euros and continued through the camp.

In the next tent, was a family who had escaped from Syria too. We spoke to a man who didn't want to give his name. His youngest son was four years old and the father pulled back his T-shirt to reveal a nasty looking scar. There had been a knife fight between two men in the camp, and the boy was unlucky enough to have been caught in the middle whilst walking around his tent. He had also been taken by another man and was only rescued when he started screaming and crying. God only knows what the man had intended to do with him. Terrifying to live in an environment like this, especially after fleeing a war torn country.

We moved to the tents pitched up on gravel in the grounds of the factory, where the heat was stifling, to the point where Rebecca and myself starting to feel ill. I think a lot of that was to do with the dust in the factory, the heat and the harrowing stories we had just heard. When we went into another tent to meet a young couple, Rebecca had to duck out as the temperature was just too much. In sweltering heat, Abdul Qader, a young hip, floppy haired man in his early twenties, told us that him and his wife had applied for an apartment to be housed in as she was 8 months pregnant but their pleas had been ignored and they were told to stay put and manage. Every person we talked to and filmed just felt desperate, helpless and hopeless, and they asked for their identities to be hidden, in case of retribution for any family members that remained in their country of origin, and also to avoid problems from camp authorities and the refugees. Rebecca managed to break the story to the world via her contacts in numerous newspapers, starting with the Business Times and followed by the Guardian, Telegraph and Independent. But there was nothing that we or anyone else could do. It really was a helpless situation.

The next day, a twenty three year old girl died in the camp of heat exhaustion.

We visited a number of camps throughout the five days we spent on the ground. Each time we met different people, mainly Syrians, Iraqis and Kurdish. Each camp was different, but the situation was the same. One camp we visited was yet another disused factory called Sanitex. I guess the name is a giveaway to what was manufactured there too. We met a number of families there, one of whom had escaped from Iraq. The father had been an engineer back home but like with everyone in every camp, they had fled with the clothes on their backs and a few bare essentials. To top it off, the men weren't allowed to work because of their refugee status, so the man's role in the family was defunct. They were just another mouth to feed and take care of for the mother, who was the centre of the family. It was soul destroying and humiliating for them, and yet again, nothing could be done about it. Another family we spoke to had endured a very dangerous sea crossing and had almost drowned. They had left because of the war, but to also get treatment for their disabled son. This too had not materialised, and the father was considering returning home with them. That's how bleak they felt.

Despite all the people's hardship including their camp suffering, everyone was still so grateful for the supplies we had delivered. However they were only just about surviving on the food being given by the camp authorities, as it was substandard food and not enough of it. This seemed to be the same in every camp we had visited and one in particular, the food supply contractor had been serving 'gone off' food, with rotten rice. Word had got back to the warehouse that people weren't eating, and were getting sick, so one of the 7.5 tonne trucks was loaded with gas bottles, gas burners and tinned and dried food in the expectation that we could help with cooking equipment that they could use to cook for themselves.

Incredulously, the truck was stopped and turned away at the camp entrance, with the camp security personnel apparently refusing to allow us to bring the food and equipment in. It was the most ridiculous bureaucratic and hostile environmental stance I had ever witnessed, and I felt like jumping out of the car and remonstrating with the police and soldiers at the camp entrance. Again, a pointless exercise in a country whose own economy had broken down and was struggling with its own issues. We turned the truck and car around and drove away from the camp. What I didn't realise was that a half a mile away from the camp, there was an olive grove, out of sight of the main entrance. The truck pulled off the road and was led across a rutted field to a clearing. It was just before sunset and a group of men and boys from inside the camp had come to meet us. They were well organised and had some radios to communicate with each other. One of them was the source of the information about the rotten food, and had rounded up two-dozen able bodied men and boys. We opened the doors of the truck and turned our heads the other way. These were human beings in need of humanitarian help. How they were going to be given it didn't matter. The truck was parked up with the doors open and everyone was allowed to take what they needed. It's a free world supposedly.

There was another vehicle who's owner shall remain nameless, that helped ferry the cargo a few hundred yards to within sight of the rear fence of the camp. I joined the throng caught up in the moment; I wanted to actually help, to do something that made a difference to their lives - blow the consequences I thought. These people are being treated worse than animals and they needed help. It was their basic human right to cook and eat good clean food, and I was going to help carry it. I was suddenly in the moment; physically and tangibly helping someone who needed food. This was a real adventure. Happening in real time! The sun was slowly setting as we carried the burners, gas bottles, tins, sacks and boxes across the most uneven undulating banks and little hills. Across a disused railway track and then into the camp itself, via a gap that had long been cut in the fence and used regularly to gain access to and from the rear of the camp. Once inside the perimeter, we set up the burners and bottles on a table hidden at the back of the camp inside an empty mess tent. We were given tea and coffee by the camp residents as they were so very grateful. We learned more about the food situation, how an external contractor was being given thirty Euros a day per person in the camp by the EU/UN to feed them. It was obvious to us all that this money wasn't being utilised anywhere near what it should have been, and the camp elders were perfectly within their rights to want to cook for themselves and their families. By the time we left the camp, it was total darkness, and we stumbled and tripped our way back across the uneven ground and headed towards the truck. Lighting our way by mobile phone, we could see that we were surrounded by a swarm of mosquitoes. In our eyes, mouths and up our noses, it was absolutely gross. After flaying our arms around, we eventually got back to the truck and car and set off to the hotel, harbouring a feeling that something had actually being accomplished and the knowledge that many more families would eat well tonight because of our efforts and teamwork.

All of the volunteers, who had paid for their own flight, hotel and food, were the ones who I took my hat off to. Nurses, teachers, financial advisors, human rights campaigners.. we all pulled together and worked hard as a unit to try to make a difference to the lives of the refugees we encountered. We had bonded and shared an experience none of us will ever forget, and to this day, we are all still in touch. There is still hope for humanity! This was my first and last aid convoy to date, but so many of the others are still organising, driving and volunteering to help Charles take the aid to the most needy, wherever they may be. I suppose, if I had to sum up this trip, my first experience of a refugee camp and the humanitarian sector, it would be like the slogan painted on the back of each of HAAD's lorries, incorporating the four humanitarian principles; *'We take Aid, not sides'*. I drove back to the UK part way with Kabir, through Albania and then Montenegro, where I stayed with him for a couple of days, taking in the picturesque medieval city of Kotor, and the warm calm Adriatic Sea. The rest of the way I was on my own, travelling through Croatia, Bosnia, Slovenia, Austria, Germany, Netherlands, Belgium and France. This gave me plenty of time to process and reflect upon what had happened over those previous ten days. The sea on one side and empty lands with 'Achtung! Minen!' (Attention! land mines!) signs not the other side, a hangover from the Balkan war; mountains and tunnels; long straight roads that went on for hours. In fact I drove 800 miles in one day. I did stop off the next day in Würzburg, Germany for lunch, to see my childhood friend James, his wife Martina and their children. His mum Kay was there visiting from the UK, so it was a welcome blast from the past and break in my solo 1800 mile journey. In the space of four days, a visit to Kotor in Montenegro and some breathtaking scenery along the way, I was back in the UK, and ready for my next assignment, but this time with a fire and sense of purpose inside of me I had never known before; to help those in need wherever they were in the world, and to share their struggles and stories far and wide. It had been a successful trip in the sense that we delivered the aid to the intended recipients and beneficiaries; I had also made the content I had envisaged, and there had been no mishaps or mess ups by me thankfully. The imposter syndrome voice had been silenced for now. The range of emotions I experienced during this trip were the full spectrum; fear, anger, love, excitement, sadness, and of course hope. Hope that humanity still has decent people who are willing to go out of their way, and even at times, put themselves in danger to help their fellow humans.

2

Little Hearts, Tanzania

'Congenital Heart Disease (CHD) is an enormous problem in Low Middle Income Countries and particularly in sub-Saharan Africa. There is an estimated 500,000 children born in Africa with CHD each year with a major proportion of this in sub-Saharan Africa. The vast majority of these children receive sub-optimal or no care at all. In East Africa: Kenya, Tanzania, and Uganda have all attempted to create a CHD service for the last 20 years with minimal success due to various factors. Visiting cardiac missions have made considerable contributions in the development of CHD services in these countries, however there remains a significant number of children with lack of care. We explore the positive aspects of the current projects, the various factors that hinder growth in this area, and what can be done to promote CHD service growth in these countries.'

Source - National Centre for Biotechnology Information, USA. (<u>Salim G. M. Jivanji</u>, <u>Sulaiman Lubega</u>, <u>Bhupi Reel</u>, and <u>Shakeel A. Qureshi</u>)

I had never been to sub-saharan Africa before and this next mission was something I didn't expect to see first hand. It was the 'Little Hearts' campaign, which had been running for a couple of years through Muntada Aid. Basically, a bunch of heart surgeons and specialists would fly into a country, set up shop and perform much needed heart operations on babies and small children. Obviously it wasn't as simple as that. The whole program was planned and overseen by Kabir, which involved finding a hospital in a country that was in need of this type of intervention, and planning the logistics of bringing the surgeons, specialist, staff and equipment to that country from Saudi Arabia. Congenital Heart Disease is especially high in this part of the world due to a multitude of factors, including chromosomal disorders, maternal infectious diseases and micro-nutrient deficiencies.

Once I had had my mandatory yellow fever jab, (some countries don't allow you in without it), we boarded our Kenyan Airlines flight at London Heathrow and flew to Dar Es'Salaam, via Nairobi.

The stop over in Nairobi was for five hours, so Kabir and I ate then tried to sleep, to no avail. The announcement "JAMBO JAMBO!" (HELLO HELLO!) then blasted over the tannoy every 15 minutes or so, making a decent snooze impossible. Finally we were called to our flight to Dar Es'Salaam, and in no time had landed and were making our way through immigration.

Outside the airport, we were picked up by one of our ground partners, a young man called Maulid. He was also filming on behalf of the ground partner and would be by my side for the next 10 days. However, there was a slight problem with accommodation. It just so happened that the exact same week, 40,000 Shia Muslim pilgrims had descended on the Tanzanian capital to commemorate Muharram, the Islamic month in which many events take place. This meant that all the affordable hotels in town had been fully booked, and the only decent hotel was 10 miles up the coast. This was a Ramada hotel so not exactly cheap, but the only one available and suitable to house working heart surgeons in air conditioned comfort. The other thing was, what should have been a twenty-minute drive took two hours to reach the hotel, due to the volume of traffic on the road, transporting the pilgrims in and around the city.

We reached the hotel, cleaned up and all met for dinner in the hotel restaurant. For those who know about the food in Ramada hotels, this won't need explaining. But for those who don't, here goes… A buffet of every type of salad you can imagine, terrines full of soups, curries, vegetables and potatoes in various forms, someone cooking the steak you have just picked, just the way you want it, chicken, lamb, paneer, goujons, steaks, frites, dauphinoise, sliced, diced, fried, seared… and that's just the starters and mains. Dessert was a whole world of colours, shapes, textures sauces, dips, fruits, meringues, cakes, jellies, creams, custards and coulis… I could go on for hours.. I did try most of it, and the halal steak was cooked to tender perfection! (I was hungry when I wrote this).

Post dinner, we met for a briefing on how the days would unfold, and what to expect. Everyone seemed very serious and focused, and rightly so for such a delicate and life saving program. As people moved off to bed after the briefing, I wandered out onto the white sandy beach with a cup of coffee and cigarette hanging out of my mouth. In front of me was the Indian ocean, waves crashing down and a really bright moon, reflecting on the water. I had another little moment, realising where I was and what I was doing there. Standing on an East African beach, in the Southern Hemisphere, about to film open heart surgery on babies. Excitement tinged with anxiety once more. Suddenly the familiar negativity from deep within muttering fear into my heart, that I would mess up somehow, but the conscious experienced part me telling myself all will be fine. InshaAllah! (God willing).

Once more into the fray, the drive to the Muhimbili Hospital in Dar Es Salaam took two hours. We arrived at the Jakaya Kikwete Cardiac Institute and met Executive Director Professor Mohammed Y. Jananbi. He showed us around the building, where the recovery ward had been set up, the operating theatre and of course the initial screening area, whose waiting room was already starting to fill up with prospective patients.

The screening room was an ultrasound machine, an electro cardiogram machine and treatment bed, where the anxious parents and their bewildered or crying children had their chest coated in gel and then their hearts scanned. There was a constant humming, beeping and swoosh swishing sound of little beating hearts coming through the ultrasound machine.

Amongst all the children, and the generic overall footage I needed for the short documentary, there were two case studies I would have to choose to follow. One catheter intervention and one open heart procedure, as explained to me by the renowned Consultant Cardiac Surgeon, Dr Mohammed Shihata, and Consultant paediatric Cardiologist, Dr Saud Bahedra. The catheter intervention involved inserting a wire mesh balloon in through an artery and into the hole and to expand the balloon, thus blocking the hole. The open heart procedure is much more complicated and involves opening the chest cavity, putting the patient onto the heart and lung machine and operating on the heart directly by hand. Both carry a risk, of varying degrees. Before this all started, I was warned not to get attached to any of the children as there was always the possibility that they may not make it past the recovery ward. This had happened in Bangladesh the year before and everyone involved was absolutely devastated. Although there is always a risk with any form of surgery, especially involving general anaesthetic, the success rate was over 95% and had generally been 100% for The Little Hearts clinics.

Once I had filmed the screening and it had been decided which children to follow, Maulid my local assistant and I spoke with the family members. The first, four year old Oningol Olassiye had travelled down from the north of Tanzania with his father Sanji. Sanji was a Masai tribesman, wore the famous black and red checked shawl and had huge stretched holes in his earlobes. The Masai tribe population is around 900,000 people, are spread across northern Tanzania and Kenya and live a semi-nomadic lifestyle. We connected straight away and it turned out that we had a lot in common. He too was forty three years old and also had four children. Two men from completely different backgrounds and parts of the world, sharing stories about our kids, laughing and connecting through facial expressions, impressions, hand gestures and non verbal communication.

The second child I would be following, open heart patient eight year old Abdul Razaq, was from Zanzibar and had come with his older sister Fatimah to get checked out. They had heard about the clinic through their local doctor and knew it was probably a once in a lifetime chance to get him help. For years now he was breathless and found it hard to move around, so this opportunity to get the help he needed was a blessing from God. The procedures were explained to them and we arranged to see them in the coming days.

We arrived back at the hotel after another two hour traffic jam, got changed and headed straight out onto the beach. The sky was clear, the sun fiercely beating down and the white sand was very hot underfoot. I had never swam in the Indian Ocean before and felt very excited about the prospect.. it seemed such a far away thing to do.. something I could have only ever dreamt of doing.. a proper travel fantasy. As I walked towards the water, the waves were medium and nothing to be fearful of. It was warm! Such an amazing feeling.. So I dived in headfirst... ahhh the crystal clear water.... And surfaced right in front of what I thought was a jellyfish. A dangerous jellyfish! It had brushed my arm and my immediate thought was to get out of the sea and pee on the sting. But the panic and fear was replaced with revulsion as the dangerous jellyfish turned out to be a bloated sea washed nappy. I turned and walked out of the water, only to see other such nappies half buried in the sand. Plastic. Fishing line. Rubbish. It was disgusting, but more than that it made me sad. The man-made pollution on such a beautiful stretch of white sandy beach and crystal clear waters. We were told that people throw rubbish and nappies from the ferry between Zanzibar and Dr Es Salaam, and they wash up on the beaches after a few days of being cleaned by the fishes and bleached by the sun. Kabir and I walked further down the beach and found a locally owned hotel next door to the Ramada. The Elephant hotel was nowhere near as plush as the Ramada, but it was clean, air-conditioned and served good clean food. The price reflected that so we decided to jump ship and book into this nice little home-from-home for the rest of our stay, saving the charity money and feeling we were helping contribute to the local economy.

That evening, we joined everyone in the main hotel for dinner; it was our last chance to dine on the fine foods, and to prepare for the first days' procedures. Again, I had no idea what I was about to experience...

*   *   *

We arrived at the Institute at 9am, and were briefed on what to expect during the day. My job was to film this first open heart procedure in its entirety, on Mohammed, one of the infants, selected the previous days. I was shown through to a locker room and given some dark blue scrubs, consisting of some drawstring trousers, a collarless tunic, white crocs, hat and face mask. Once dressed, I had to 'scrub' my hands, face and forearms with surgical soap. The camera was cleaned with disinfectant antiseptic wipes and I was shown into the operating theatre. The theatre was another mass of humming, bleeping machines with a big clock on the wall, and a machine that looked like something from Dr Who's Tardis. This was the heart and lung machine. A magical device that kept the patient alive whilst the heart was being worked on, by taking the blood and oxygenating it and pushing it back into the arteries. I was in absolute awe of the science behind it.

Feeling very anxious and nervous, I made sure I stayed well away from the operating table so as not to get in the way. Dr Shihata was performing the operation and straight away told me to come closer so I could get the shots I needed. He put me at ease immediately and told me to enjoy witnessing something most people will never see in their lifetime. From start to finish, the procedure must have taken five hours. Five hours that flew by.. from the initial incision to stitching up the fixed patient, I was totally immersed as the morning unfolded. But it's not a pretty sight. The chest is cut open with a scalpel, then the chest bone and rib cage is cut and cracked open to allow access to the heart and lungs. It's a very messy business, and I could feel myself trembling as I witnessed a tiny beating heart right in front of my eyes. Once the patient is hooked up to the heart and lung machine, a puffing clicking whirring device, the heart is then ready to be operated on. Seeing the incredibly delicate and fine work of stitching up a hole in the heart is truly breathtaking. The skill and precision needed is awe inspiring, and once the required work has been done, the arteries are reconnected to the heart from the heart and lung machine and the heart restarted. This is done with the tiniest of paddles, almost like salad spoons, and a small voltage is used to jump start the heart. Then the chest and ribcage is closed, wired together and the chest sewn up. When Mohammed was wheeled into the intensive care recovery unit, I managed to relax a little. The procedure had been a success and he was groggy and awake not long after. This part of the operation was critical to monitor the patients recovery, vital statistics and to make sure that fluid and blood was drained away to allow healing and a full recovery. I had lost my sense of smell in a rugby accident in 2011, so I can generally film anywhere and not be affected by the smell. However, by the time I left the operating theatre, all I could taste was iodine and burnt flesh and bone from the laser scalpel used. After a scrub down, mouth wash and plenty of water gargling on my part, we all headed to the roof of the hospital for lunch.

The view from on top of the hospital was amazing. It was in the shade, due to being covered by a large roof like canopy, but we could see out across Dar es-Salaam. There were eagles, vultures, ravens, butterflies, and all kinds of birds and insects. Before us was a buffet of rice, mutton, fish, and fruit but I just couldn't get the taste of iodine and burnt flesh from my mouth. That day I didn't touch any meat.

The afternoon's procedure went equally as well and by sundown, we were pulling into the hotel car park. Kabir and I wandered next door to the Elephant hotel and had an early night, exhausted from the mental and physical intensity of the first day.

Today's procedure was the catheter intervention on Oningol, the four year old boy from the Masai tribe. He seemed very relaxed when we met him in the preparation area. However his father Sanji was quite the opposite. I could see the fear in his eyes, knowing that this was a serious operation, yet not knowing what to expect. All was calm until the anaesthetist came to give Oningol his anaesthetic. Big needle being pushed into the back of his hand, he understandably screamed and cried, and within less than thirty seconds, he was still. Scrubbed up once more, and now wearing a lead overcoat to block the radiation of the X-ray machine being used. I followed the nurse carrying him to the operating table. Again, the room was packed with the highest technology in this kind of medical intervention. The biggest difference was that the work being done was via a small incision in the groin area and the stent, a wire mesh balloon was fed up and along the artery into the hole in the heart. This was monitored by the use of X-ray machines so the surgeon could watch the progress. Once in place, the stent or wire mesh balloon was opened and left in place to fill the hole. The procedure didn't take anywhere near as long and within a couple of hours, Oningol was back in the recovery room. The operation was a success and the relief on the face of Sanji, I will never forget. His gratitude and humility for the Little Hearts program was clear to see, and it was a truly humbling moment, especially when Oningol woke up and saw his dad's face. They left the same day and I swapped numbers with Sanji. He didn't have his own mobile phone, but had borrowed a friends. We were going to keep in touch for sure, but as so often in life, this never materialised and we never spoke again.

It had been a few days since I had filmed the first open heart surgery of this clinic, and these days had been filled with various operations, interviews and even a location shoot at the home of one of the children, somewhere in the red earthed hills outside of Dar Es-Salaam. I had Maulid with me, assisting on these shoots and he was a very helpful and resourceful young man. I asked him what made him become a film maker for this particular program but he always answered with 'It's good work alhamdulillah'. Whenever we were at the hospital, he was always on hand to help translate from Swahili to English for me, and it was whilst interviewing Abdul Razaq and his sister, prior to his open heart procedure, I made the very mistake I had been warned about. I made a connection with Abdul Razaq. He reminded me of my eldest son. His open faced smile was so infectious, and his general demeanour was so relaxed. In retrospect, this relaxed demeanour may have been due to the lack of energy through his heart condition. We talked, smiled, rolled a football to each other, high fived and just hit it off. His sister Fatimah had brought him over from Zanzibar when she heard of this clinic through a friend. For years he had been pale, lethargic, and breathless when he tried even the simplest of exercises. He had been this way since birth, and his health and physical state was deteriorating. His heart was not able to work hard enough to keep his body and blood oxygenated and his prognosis was for a very short life. During the screening, I had overheard a conversation saying what I thought was him having a 70% chance of survival from this procedure. I had misheard it completely. Because there were three procedures needed on his heart at the same time, and due to him being almost nine years old, he was given a 70% chance of *not* surviving the operation. I was made aware of this just before the nurse carried him through to the theatre. He was smiling all the way and then he was asleep, mouth taped to an oxygen airway and laid out, ready to start.

I couldn't watch the incision, or the chest being cracked open. I just filmed close-ups of Dr Shihata, the faces of the nurses and support staff, trying not to think that it was Abdul Razaq on the operating table. After a while, I filmed parts of the procedure. He needed to have three areas of his heart fixed, and by this time, I had calmed down, and was hopeful. Watching the delicate pieces of plastic being stitched to the holes in the heart, I was amazed at the intricate stitching being done by Dr Shihata. All three parts of the operation had been successful, and his arteries removed from the heart and lung machine and his heart reconnected. Now it was time to restart the heart with the 'Salad spoons', as I called them. I was expecting it to happen straight away, as with the first procedure I had filmed. But nothing happened. Dr Shihata asked for the voltage to be increased... and nothing. Again, an increase in the voltage... nothing. I started to panic. I felt sick. My heart was in my throat. How could he come through all of this only to not survive at the end? I could feel my eyes start to well up. In my heart and mind, I was pleading with God to bring him through this. Please let his heart restart! Another rise in voltage. Nothing. A flat line whine..... I could feel the anxiety building in the room and finally Dr Shihata pushed the voltage up some more and gave it another go. Click. Click. Beeeeeeeeeeeeeeep...............Beep. Beep. Beep. Beep. I wanted to cry. I felt sick. I felt relieved and almost elated. His heart was beating again. Alhamdulillah!!! Dr Shihata and his team had pulled off the almost impossible. Such testament to his skill and the dedication of him and his team. I followed Abdul Razaq through to the recovery ward and waited with him until he regained consciousness.

The next day we went to see Abdul Razaq and his sister Fatimah. He was awake and sat up in bed, smiling. Of course he was smiling. He always smiled. Fatimah explained how grateful she was for Muntada Aid and Little Hearts and that they had saved her little brother's life. This is when Maulid called me to one side and told me to ask him again why he did this work and was involved in this project. So I asked him. He pulled up his t-shirt to show a long scar across his chest. He too had undergone this operation as a child. I was gobsmacked. For him to see what had happened to him as a child must have taken such strength of character. It took on such a symbolic meaning for me, and Maulid ended up doing the translation voice over for Fatimah's interview on the film I made.

The trip ended with a dinner at the Ramada hotel, with the Donors from RAF, the Royal Family of Qatar charity fund. Speeches were given, photos taken and we all said our goodbyes.

This was another life changing mission, and the dedication and generosity of all involved, especially the donors RAF, Dr Shihata, Dr Bahendra and all the staff is testament to the good that can be done in the world. There have been other heart operation missions by other charities and hospitals in previous years at various locations around the world, however some of these have sent trainee surgeons as well as surgeons; a disgraceful action in my opinion, and ethically unforgivable. With Little Hearts however, all the heart surgeons and staff were fully trained and highly skilled and experienced. Of the twenty one open heart surgery operations and twenty nine catheter interventions, being fifty in total, they were each and every one a total success.

I had witnessed something most people will never see in their lifetime, and the adrenaline and uncertainty of such life or death operations took a while to abate. It was an adventure of a different kind, but it left me feeling the fragility of human life even more acutely.

I learned a lot of lessons on this trip, and one in particular, which is probably the saddest of all, is don't get attached to the people you are serving. You can care and support and help, but that's it. At the end of the day, we are humanitarians and need to adhere to the four principles of humanity, neutrality, impartiality and independence. There is no room for emotions, although this isn't always the case with the human condition, as I have repeatedly found on this journey. It is easier said than done, and I will always remember the angelic smile of Abdul Razaq, sat up on in his bed, grateful for the new lease of life Little Hearts has given him.

3

New Life and Broken Minds, Turkey

'Turkey continues to host the largest number of refugees worldwide, as the number of people forcibly displaced across the world due to conflict, violence and persecution hit record levels. Turkey currently hosts some 3.6 million registered Syrian refugees along with close to 320,000 persons of concern from other nationalities.'

Source - UNHCR

I landed in Antakya airport early in the morning, after a connecting flight from Istanbul. Nestling in Hatay, the southern most region of Turkey, Kirikhan sat 12km from the Syrian border and 75km from Aleppo. There had been a massive influx of refugees over the last few years, and many of them were orphans. The need for a safe environment for these children was vital, so Muntada Aid had built the 'New Life Orphanage'; a small orphan complex attached to a newly built school. There were local children attending and the majority of them were from Aleppo. I had literally landed, having not slept a wink, checked my suitcase into the hotel and went straight across the road to film the opening ceremony of the orphanage. It was a grand affair with local TV crews and dignitaries sat in the November sun, cutting ribbons, presenting trophies and glassware, and opening the doors for a guided tour. Many of the children had moved in with their grandmothers or mothers. In Islam, an orphan is a child who loses their father or mother, and most of these children had lost either one or both. The status of orphans in Islam is also very high and important; the Prophet Muhammad (peace be upon him) was an orphan and helping an orphan is very rewarded. There is a Hadith (saying or story of the Prophet Muhammad (peace be upon him)) which states the following:

> *Narrated Sahl bin Sa`d: The Prophet (ﷺ) said, "I and the person who looks after an orphan and provides for him, will be in Paradise like this," putting his index and middle fingers together.*
>
> Source: Sahih al-Bukhari 6005

Tariq Shaikh, head of fundraising for Muntada, had been there a couple of days in advance to help oversee the final touches. We went from room-to-room to speak to the orphans and their carers, and in each room there was a tray of strong sweet black tea or Turkish coffee. For the previous year, I had abstained from caffeine, as I had started to get anxiety attacks, so when offered a strong coffee, I politely declined. Tariq pointed out to me that this would offend due to Syrian culture, and insisted I accept. Not wanting to upset our host, I thanked her and sipped at the small piping hot glass of strong black coffee. It was actually a warm welcome after a sleepless flight. We moved to the next apartment in the complex and the same thing happened. Again, I accepted the drink and half an hour later we had moved on. Eight apartments, five coffees and three teas later, we had finished our rounds and I was buzzing. Amazingly, because I was so focused on filming, and listening to the stories of these children, I didn't have time to let the anxiety kick in. I was hooked once more on caffeine and it was delightful.

Our time in Kirikhan was very short and we only had time to film a few case study stories. One of which was for a boy called Ahmed, around ten years of age, very short with sandy red hair and freckles. His parents had both died in Aleppo, and he had just moved into the *New Life* Orphanage with his grandmother, and they were both full of gratitude for their new home. His story was like that of so many others. One morning his mother had gone to the market, and there had been a barrel bomb attack. When she hadn't returned, and his father had heard no word from her, he himself went to the

27

market to try to find her. That's when the helicopter returned and dropped another barrel bomb. In the space of an hour, Ahmed lost both his parents, becoming an orphan. He and his grandmother fled Aleppo and made it over the border to Turkey. They had been staying in an old derelict cottage on the edge of town, with no electricity or running water. We visited the old house and filmed him walking around it, pointing out where he used to sleep, wash and where they ate. This time of year got very cold, and the air was filled with acrid smoke, as residents burned wood, coal and whatever they could get their hands on. There were thousands of refugees living in the town in varying conditions, so for Ahmed and his grandmother, the *New Life* orphanage was a blessing. Not only did they have a safe, warm, clean and secure place to live, Ahmed could also get an education, which in turn could give him a better life outside of the poverty, and help his family and society in future. The knock on effect education has to a region or nation is vital to build a more stable economy and environment.

There were other children and grandparents we spoke to and filmed case studies of, and for each of them, this orphanage truly meant a new life for them, even though the trauma and loss of their parents is something that will probably never heal fully. Our Syrian translator Ibrahim had been an English teacher before the war, in Hama, a city halfway between Aleppo and Homs. He was talking to a young girl and suddenly had to stop. He swiftly stood up and left the room. I went after him to see what was wrong, and he was sobbing, tears rolling down his cheeks. It was heartbreaking to see. I asked him what had happened, and he told me that the girl had been describing her house back in Syria, the cedar trees, flowers, gardens full of fruit trees and how she one day wished to return. It was too much for him. Recalling his own house back in Hama, the family he left behind, members killed and the desperation of fleeing a war torn country. He didn't want the girl to see him crying, just in case it reminded her of the horrors and losses she had experienced. No words I could say would make him feel better, so I put my arm on his shoulder and gently squeezed. After a moment, he wiped his face, composed himself and returned, with a smile on his face, the girl unaware of his pain and sadness. Even in his own situation of being a refugee, having lost everything himself, he kept his professionalism, empathy and consideration at the forefront, not wishing to cause the girl any pain or sadness herself. Such selflessness, I wondered if I would have had the maturity and sense of awareness of others feelings over my own. It was one of the many valuable lessons I have learned on the trips; no matter how I am feeling or how it affects me emotionally, I need to remain composed in front of those I am helping or serving. There will always be a time and place to process my own stuff, but not in front of those who have suffered trauma upon trauma.

Our hosts took us out for dinner on the last night, we drank sweet tea, ate Turkish sweets and talked until late. The next morning, we boarded a flight for Istanbul.

*　　*　　*

This was my first time in Istanbul itself. I had passed through the airport on my way to Antakya so this was a real treat. The cab drive from the airport took in the Bosphorus on our right, and on our left were Hagia Sofia and the Blue Mosque. We drove up a hill and turned right into an area called the Fatih district, next to the beautiful Fatih Mosque. We checked into our hotel, then walked up to the Fatih mosque in time for Dhuhr prayer. The surrounding grounds were beautiful and the Architecture of the exterior of the mosque was very grand. The interior was totally breathtaking. Windows upon windows, high up into the domed ceiling. Geometric patterns, Islamic scriptures, arches, inlaid stonework… just beautiful. The atmosphere was so serene and the Mosque wasn't anywhere near full, but at least half of the vast expansive red carpet was covered with worshippers. We prayed, and then went for lunch in the Syrian quarter on the other side of the courtyard. We knew the food was going to be good because it was packed with locals. Eventually we got a table at the back and feasted on a medley of delights; grilled meats, fried cheese sticks, hummus, babaganoush to name but a few.

After lunch we walked down into the city to *Broken Minds*, another Muntada Aid project, the steep streets branching off left and right from the main road. We turned into an unassuming shop door which was the hub for the project. The project itself was amazing. Each child had a therapist assigned to them. They were sat around a table and asked to draw something from their past. Either something they had witnessed, something they feared or what they would like to happen. It was startling to see the drawings after the session. Pictures of helicopters dropping what looked like barrel bombs onto houses. Body parts and blood, soldiers shooting stick families. Burning buildings, explosions and one particularly graphic drawing of a man in a suit and hat being shot and stabbed in the head and body. This, I was told, was Bashir Al Assad, the Syrian president. It was what one seven year old child wanted to do to him. The fear, trauma, anguish and anger was evident in all of the drawings. But how could drawing such things help these children, damaged mentally, emotionally and sometimes physically? The therapy was very well thought through. Combined with psychiatrists, touch therapy, sports therapy and play therapy, the children were slowly being taught how to be children again. The importance of such a program could shape a country for generations to come.

The centre also helped to teach the children how to speak Turkish so they could attend school eventually, and also it provided help with asylum seeking, official papers and getting help from the relevant authorities. One of the children in the centre, Mariam, had drawn a picture of a helicopter gunship shooting up a house. This was her house back in Aleppo. Half of her family had been wiped out, with her mother and father surviving. The trauma had been too much and she had withdrawn into herself. As we left for our hotel, we were told that Mariam would be found on the street at night, selling tissues to survive and supporting her family as her father couldn't work due to his injuries from the shooting. We headed out later that night to try to find her, but she was nowhere to be found.

The next morning, we took a cab to her home address where her parents had agreed to let us come to film them as a case study. We were welcomed in by her mother at first, and eventually her father came in and spoke to us at length. He was embarrassed, felt totally helpless and carried a lot of shame around the fact that he couldn't provide for his family through his injury, and feared for Mariam's safety, being out on the streets at night selling tissues. Anything could happen to her. I stopped filming as he broke down crying. In order to divert attention, as we were all sat together in the one living area, I called Mariam over and handed her my camera. I showed her how to take a photo and let her click away. My Canon 7d has a bit of weight to it and even I struggle at times, so to see this tiny and thin child swinging it around and snapping was a sight to behold. Her mum stopped and stared, placing her hand on her husbands arm. They both looked at Mariam, then at each other, then at me. She was smiling and laughing for the first time, in as long as they could both remember. It was yet another humbling and heartwarming moment that I was lucky enough to share, and will never forget!

After we returned to the office, we covered a few case studies and the donor feedback documentation was taken by Tariq. The help given to these families was invaluable on so many levels, and support was put in place to help Maryam and her family to negate the need for her being at risk, selling tissues on the streets a night.

With the work finished, Tariq generously offered to treat me to a Turkish Hamam. I had no idea what that was, but I was up for the challenge. His gleeful, cheeky grin broke through, as we entered an old stone doorway; and descended the steps into what I would call an old Turkish bath. He knew what we were in store for, and was no doubt chuckling to himself for what I was about to experience for the first time. We put our shorts on, showered and made our way into the first area, some kind of pool. It's all a bit of a blur to be honest, but what did stick in my mind was the hands-on treatment we received. We both entered an antique, ornate, high-ceiling room and laid out on two stone tables. There was some kind of rubber matting on them so it wasn't too uncomfortable. I felt a bit concerned when two large gentlemen with huge pot bellies, handlebar moustaches and towels wrapped around their waists came in and asked us to lie on our fronts. It turned out that these were official hamam massage guys and they were literally there to bust us up; bending, pulling, slapping and finally a soap-filled rough mitten to rub the skin down. But he wasn't quite finished. My guy walked off, just as I was actually *relaxing,* and he returned and threw a bucket of ice cold water over me; I screamed like a girl! Nothing wrong with that, but it had them all in stitches, Tariq included. Post massage, we had our feet, heads and hands wrapped in hot towels with essential oils. It was a real treat and I was forever grateful to brother Tariq.

We flew home the following day, and what I reflected on, was the absolute *necessity* for both projects we had visited; *New Life* Orphanage and Broken Minds. There is a whole generation of Syrians who need such vital therapy as this, but will never get it. Such trauma becomes generational trauma and can mould a nation or people. It's not just Syrian either; the need for this kind of therapy is worldwide, and especially in conflict zones, and countries where people have faced genocide.

Tariq and I had not always worked harmoniously in the office, probably due to our different ways of working, but in the field he was my brother. It is said that the best way to get to know a person is to live with them or travel with them. I had been lucky enough to get to know and see the 'real' man I was working with; dedicated, generous, honest and enthusiastic. Human interaction is definitely one of the many blessings of this job, and I was given a real lesson in humility and care of others on this trip.

**Since this chapter was written, Turkey has experienced the worst earthquake in its history with more than 50,000 people killed and millions now homeless. Kirikhan was one of the worst hit cities, with half of those dead in the Hatay and Kirikhan province. I returned there on an earthquake emergency mission in April 2023 and the devastation was extensive. Miraculously, all of the Syrian families in the New Life Orphanage have survived, but I have no news about our translator Ibrahim, or the other helpers and staff. May Allah bless them and keep them safe Ameen.

4

Emergency Response, Somaliland

'Between the years 2016 and 2017 Somalia faced one of its most severe droughts due to consecutive poor rainy seasons which pushed the country to the brink of famine with over half of the population in desperate need of assistance. The drought triggered crop failure and high levels of livestock deaths and sickness. Towns and villages were painted with dots of animal carcasses from one corner to the other.'

Source - ICRC

In March 2017, and after a fascinating and educational ten months and three life changing trips with Muntada Aid, I left and became a videographer for the Wakefield based charity, Penny Appeal. My experiences at Muntada were golden, but due to them being such a small charity, the budget just wasn't there for as many foreign assignments as I had hoped for. Penny Appeal needed plenty of filming done prior to Ramadan, so I joined them at just the right time.

My first trip was an emergency response, delivering food and water to remote villages in the drought hit region of Burco in Eastern Somaliland. This was going to be my first 'Scary' mission. I looked at the foreign office website and the whole of Somalia and Somaliland was coloured red. Do not visit under any circumstances. I soon learned that if one listened to the foreign office, they would never get out of bed, let alone leave the house! Somaliland had become independent from Somalia in 1991 after a civil war. It had previously been known as British Somaliland. It was, or so I was told, a much safer place than Somalia itself and its capital city, Mogadishu.

I had to go to the Somaliland Embassy in Whitechapel, East London with Elsa, the French program officer in charge of this particular relief distribution. Walking up and down the Whitechapel road, looking for a flag or some kind of sign or insignia of the Embassy, we walked into what seemed like a small mall. Down the stairs and set in an office at the end of the corridor, was the Embassy of Somaliland. We were met by a larger than life gentleman called Shaikh Adam Hassan. Shaikh Adam had an orangey grey beard, a radiant smile and an air of kindness and a sense of gravitas. He helped us get our visas there and then, and said he would meet us in Hargaisa, the Somaliland capital in a few days. Elsa and I went over a few last details together, where she made a point of telling me that I'd need to change terminal once I had landed in Dubai, but there should be enough time for the transfer. She was flying from Manchester, and I from London Heathrow, and we would meet there and travel onwards together.

Within 48 hours I was on my way to Dubai on an evening flight, and after almost six hours in the air, I was feeling the need for a cigarette quite badly. As soon as we landed, and I had passed through the onward journey security check, I headed for the smoking room. These odd little rooms in many airports around the world are generally full of smokers, and the the air is thick with smoke. In some airports, there is no real ventilation so ones eyes sting with the amount of smoke in there. This one in Dubai wasn't so bad, and it was about thirty minutes and a few cigarettes later that I looked on the board for my flight number. It was nowhere to be seen. I connected to the airport WIFI and a few messages popped up on my phone. They were from Elsa; 'Have you landed yet?', 'Are you on your way to terminal 3?', 'We haven't got much time!'... I panicked and remembered what Elsa had said about getting to another terminal. I looked at the time and realised I had less than an hour to get to where i needed to be. Running through the airport, I finally found the right bus and hopped on but it sat there, not moving. I tapped on the window of the driver cab and he just ignored me. Eventually, it set off, slowly driving around the airport grounds, under terminals, across runways, around parked aircraft, and it even stopped at another terminal to pick more people up. It took an age of twenty minutes to get to terminal three, but I made it just in time. Elsa was stood there by the gate just as it was about to shut. We made the flight by the skin of our teeth, which luckily was only a quarter full, giving me a whole row of seats to stretch out and sleep in. We were in the air and on our way to Hargeisa.

Somaliland was hot. Very hot. Almost 38ºC at eight o'clock in the morning.. kinda hot. We stopped at a hotel for some refreshments and met with the fundraiser/presenter on this trip, Riz. As we were foreigners, and I was a white European, and more unusually, Elsa a white European female, it was compulsory for us to have an armed policeman accompany us for the duration of the trip for our own safety. The three of us, with Shaikh Adam and the police officer with an AK47 set off to our destination town called Burco, pronounced *'BUR-O'*. To get from Hargeisa to Burco was going to be a four-hour drive through the desert. It didn't make sense on the map, as we had to drive northeast towards the seaside city of Berbera, then head south east to Burco. When I asked Shaikh Adam why we couldn't drive directly, he said there were no roads and it would take a day at least.

The drive was cramped and uncomfortable, and the roads quite insane. Trucks and cars, driving on the wrong side of the road to avoid deep craters and potholes in the cracked and rutted tarmac. Every ten or so kilometres, there was a checkpoint with a soldier. We would have to show I.D. and then drive on. Most of these checkpoint guards had what looked like cricket balls inside their mouths, and red eyes. This was down to the local custom of chewing Khat. Khat is a plant with green leaves, similar to the coca plant of South America and is a stimulant similar to cocaine and with the ability to stave off hunger and tiredness. What it did do was make these guys jumpy, strung out and paranoid. Not a great combination, when coupled with a baking hot sun and semi automatic weapons. Dotted all over the landscape were termite hills. Strange twisted human like figures, like unfinished sculptures or half built giant sand castles.

This felt like a real adventure. Even now, on my fourth mission, I was checking in with myself on how adventurous this really was. Not many people I knew from days of old would have experienced something like this. I wondered what my old schoolmates and the bullies would think of me now? The guys from my raving days; Old bosses and former employers; Would this trip truly validate me as an adventurer? Would they be impressed? Another checkpoint jolted me back to reality and I suddenly felt foolish for having such thoughts. *'Look at where you are and what you're doing?!'* I thought to myself. This is as real as it gets.

We stopped in Berbera for lunch, and then drove up through the mountains on hairpin bends and long queues of traffic stuck behind lorries belching out black acrid smoke. As we crossed the top of the mountains, the view of the arid plain was laid out for as far as the eye could see. There were what I thought were plumes of dust from jeeps or trucks driving at various places and it seemed a well populated area. However, these plumes were actually dust devils; small tornados of sand and dust, whipped up by the hot dry air and spinning them across the landscape.

After four hours, we arrived in Burco. A small city with sand and dust covering everything. Low levels buildings; shops; homes; all mixed in with each other. We checked into the Egal hotel, dropped our bags and set straight out into the desert to a remote community who were going to receive a truck load of food aid. The road, if it could be called that, was sand compacted into track marks by the few vehicles that passed that way, and along the side of the road and in the surrounding brushlands, were dead animals; camels, goats, cattle.. having all had died from hunger, thirst and sickness caused by such harsh unforgiving drought conditions? This meant that the animals were inedible and were just decomposing where they fell and it was so hot and arid, that most of the carcasses looked mummified rather than rotting.

It took us a hour or so to reach the village. As we pulled in, I could see the whole community waiting to greet us. I was expecting a mad frenzy at the back of the aid truck, as I had witnessed in one refugee camp in Greece, but no. It couldn't have been more different. The men were all sat one side of the truck and the women on the other. The children were all running around, playing and visibly excited at what was about to happen. To the rear of the truck, individual stacks of rice, pulses, oil, tinned food, salt and spices were spaced out, across the ground. Shaikh Adam's staff had a list of names, and each one was called out, one at a time. Calmly, quietly and with dignity, each person's name was called to collect their items, and then carry them back to their homes. I followed and filmed a boy and a girl in their mid teens as they carried their items home, and I pitched in carrying a sack of rice. The rice sat on my shoulder and my camera in my other hand, we walked between two small stone shacks, past a large swathe of brushwood and into their home, made from sticks and tarpaulin. Inside was an elderly grandmother, with shiny leathery skin and a bright red hijab. I think she was surprised to see me. I don't think that a sunburned white man was an everyday sight there, so not wanting to freak her out, I gave my Salaams, quickly took some photos, and returned back to the distribution. Within a couple of hours, our work was done, and we headed back to the town of Burco.

As we drove, the sun was setting and by chance (or planning on Shaikh Adam's part) we stopped at a small, square stone mosque by the side of the dusty track. The Adhan (call to prayer) was being called through a crackly speaker, which was powered by a car battery.. which in turn also powered the lights in the mosque. We made our ablutions and then joined in the prayer. It felt completely surreal, to be in the desert, in a tiny stone mosque, praying with strangers I had never met. This however, became commonplace for me over the next few years, and is another beautiful aspect of Islam and travelling. We stand shoulder to shoulder with strangers in a mosque, and pray as brothers in Islam. Alhamdulillah!

The next morning, Shaikh Adam came with some fresh roti cooked by his wife and we sat down to a breakfast of omelette, fried eggs, oranges and coffee. Once more, the temperature was pushing forty degrees, and we set off to where the water pump and tankers were. A total of ten tankers were lined up in a big open area of wasteland, and each was filled with water from a huge holding tank thirty metres up on a tower. This was being constantly replenished by the chug chugging of a generator pump, pulling the water from aquifers hundreds of metres down. Once all were full, each truck peeled off towards their respective destinations and departed for various villages around the region. We followed one to a small remote village, about forty five minutes drive from Burco. As the tanker pulled off the road and into the desert, we could see around fifty or so villagers, each with 10 gallon water cans, awaiting the delivery. Suddenly I had an idea - wouldn't it be great to actually ride in on the back of the tanker, filming a long perspective down the tankers side as we pulled up to the water holding tank? So without considering the dangers, that's what I did. I jumped up on the back and hung off at a 45 degree angle, holding onto the rear ladder, red dust flying in the air from the wheels of the truck thundering through the arid desert plain; getting the shot I wanted and casting a stark contrast between the red of the dust, the white of the tanker and the blue of the sky. I loved it, but was told afterwards that it was irresponsibly dangerous, could have ended badly and definitely wasn't on the risk assessment form! I got a cracking shot though and I said I'd do it again if I had to… which I did a year later in Yemen.

The water holding tank was a concrete lined square pit, dug into the sand, with wires and thorny brushwood covering it to stop animals from wandering or falling in. The hose was lowered in and the tank started to fill. Riz did his presenting to camera, and then I filmed some of the villagers filling up their canisters, with children playing around in the water. It was amazing to see how the people living there had to rely upon a tanker of water due to the drought, whereas all we had to do back home is turn on a tap, and fresh, cold and clean water flows out. This was one of the many things I had taken for granted my entire life, until I saw it first hand. Water is life and too many people around the world don't have access to any water, let alone clean drinking water, yet there is enough money, technology and ability to provide this vital resource if humanity so desired.

After the distribution, we visited a garden built by Shaikh Adam where mangoes, limes, peppers, and other fruits and vegetables grew, thanks to an irrigation system he had built. It was a small oasis in the arid desert. And there were plenty of camels wandering around freely. By this point, patches on my arms and neck were badly sunburned due to my hasty application of sun screen earlier that day. I returned to the vehicle to rehydrate and took on some water. Shaikh Adam gave me my first taste of raw, unpasteurised camel milk, which didn't taste of much at the time of drinking, but the strong after taste of goat-like cheesy-ness just couldn't be shaken. However my sense of taste is not what it should be due to losing my sense of smell, so perhaps any subtleties of flavour were lost on my crude palette..

We pulled off in the Toyota Landcruiser 80 series, and headed for the road via a shortcut. This SUV was amazing. A 3.8 litre turbo diesel, it sounded like a turbo charged lorry engine, and bounced in and out of sandy hollows that any other vehicle would have been stuck in. It was a lot of fun and soon we were back in Burco. We stopped at a hospital there and were shown around one of the malnutrition wards. It was pretty shocking. Babies with flies around their eyes and mouths, stomachs distended and bloated, arms and legs so skinny and almost skeletal features. Anxious mothers were sat with them, helpless, and just having to wait to see if their children would survive. Their skinny wrists, hands and arms hooked up to saline drips and and it was heartbreaking to see. The doctor said that these were the lucky ones, as half the children with malnutrition being brought in from remote villages, would die on the journey to the hospital. Such tragedy that could be avoided. It gave me an idea to plan a road trip with vehicles from the UK, to Somaliland to be used as mobile medical units to assist the local communities. This plan turned into a proposal to make a six-part TV series of the overland drive. It got to the meeting stage, but sadly never made it past that, due to budget constraints, red tape and some unfortunate egos within the charity.

We checked out of the hotel and hit the road for our four hour night time drive back to Hargeisa. The first half of the drive was fine, apart from swerving to miss trucks on the wrong side of the road, doing their pot hole dances. Checkpoints came and went, and before long, I had drifted off in the back seat. I was woken to bright lights and bustling people. We had arrived in Berbera once more, the port town on the Gulf of Aden. Shaikh Adam led us into a restaurant and out into the back garden. It was warm, beautiful, with moths and mosquitos everywhere and the sound of the sea crashing onto the beach thirty metres away. The food was delicious and the sweet coffee hit the spot. Asking where the bathroom was, I was pointed in the direction of a small block and nervously made my way over there. It was worse than I thought. I swung the door open and there was a hole in the ground, a tap and a small watering can. Now as I write this today, it's no great shakes as I have experienced this and worse many times on my travels, but at this time it was my first experience. Needless to say, I made it out unscathed.

The second leg of the road trip back to Hargeisa was the same, until we reached yet another checkpoint about twenty kilometres outside the city. There was a truck waiting at the checkpoint and it was taking forever, so Shaikh Adam decided to pull around in front of it. This startled the already strung-out guard, and he lifted his gun and pointed it at us. This was the first time I had *ever* had a gun pointed at me, and although it was brief, it was pretty scary. In fact, I think I was equally angry as scared, that someone who was visibly wired with bulging red eyes would have the audacity to point something so bloody dangerous at anyone, let alone me. What if he fired it, or it went off by mistake? The soldier came round to Shaikh Adam and started yelling at him. He was visibly high from chewing Khat and very agitated. Shaikh Adam just laughed and told him to calm down, which didn't help the situation. After a minute of chuckling to himself in the face of the wired soldier, shouting and waving his arms and gun around, Shaikh Adam drove off and we continued on our journey, a little more awake than before. *'That was pretty adventurous'* I thought.

Arriving in one piece, we stayed in a hotel near the airport, where Riz and I edited our film of the last couple of days and uploaded to the charity website. In the early hours and after a couple of hours sleep, Shaikh Adam dropped us to the airport and we said our farewells. We went through security. And then we went through it again. And a third time. I had never experienced security at this level. Every item of kit, I had to power up or switch on, show its use, then pack it away. Every item was X-rayed and swabbed and checked and double-checked. Once they were satisfied that all was safe, we sat in the bare departure room awaiting the flight back to Dubai. We had been on the ground for a total of thirty-six action packed hours, and had seen and experienced many things in that time. It took a lot longer to digest it all, and alongside making it out without being shot, I was grateful to have been a part of this whirlwind trip.

5

Abdul Mateen

'Vision 2020 - ''The right to Sight'' global campaign to eliminate avoidable blindness by the year 2020.

Blindness is one of the major health care problems in Bangladesh. About 0.75 million people are blind, including 40,000 children, which are avoidable through proper treatment and care. Bangladesh is enjoying the unique status among few other countries to ratify the Vision 2020; which is a meaningful step towards achieving the goals of Vision 2020.'

Source - WHO / Bangladesh National
Council For The Blind

After a brief trip to Senegal and Gambia filming at orphanages and water wells, I headed off to Bangladesh for the first time. I was flying on my 44th birthday, on my own to meet Riz, Craig and Irfan Rajput in Dhaka and for a few projects dotted around the country. The emirates flight was a long daytime one, and on the second leg from Dubai to Dhaka, I had the back half of the plane to myself. After we had taken off, I noticed that the seat belt was covered in snot, so I asked the flight attendant to move me to another seat. I mentioned that it was my birthday and tried to get a cheeky upgrade to business class. That didn't work, but I was moved to the back row of the plane and told I could stretch out over the four seats. After lunch, I eventually drifted off to sleep.

Upon waking, the same flight attendant said to me 'Mr Robinson, could you come with me please?', and asked me to follow her into the galley at the back of the plane. I thought to myself,

'What have I done?'. We were met by four other attendants, a happy birthday banner and a slice of cake from first class. It was such a lovely gesture, and we all posed for photos and talked for the remainder of the flight.

Dhaka airport was hot, humid and very busy. It took an hour or so to get the visa on arrival, and finally make it out to collect my bags. I had the hotel address and was told to jump in a taxi and make my own way. The ride took almost two hours to go from the airport to the hotel downtown. No air conditioning and a thunderstorm was brewing, the air almost yellow and close. This was my first experience of the traffic in Dhaka, and it was insane, and I describe it in more detail later on. I checked in and met Irfan and Riz on the roof of the hotel at the restaurant, and spoke to Irfan properly for the first time. I had no idea that this man would become like my big brother, and one of the very few people I trust with my life. The air was thick and heavy and in the distance, lightening flashed and thunder rolled out across the city, sending us inside as the torrential rain started to pour down.

The strangest thing happened just before bed. I had showered, prayed and was tucking in under the covers, when I heard a voice outside my window. Ignoring it and putting it down to jet lag, I switched off the lights and turned over to sleep. After all, I was on the 13th floor and there were no balconies on this side of the hotel. Then I heard it again. This time I saw a glow outside the window ledge. Jumping up and opening the curtains, there was a man, rope around his waist, on the phone, talking to someone I presume about changing the lightbulb he had in his other hand. It was so bizarre and random. This was my introduction to how many random and unexpected things happen in Bangladesh. I left the guy to it and went to sleep.

The next day was a free day as Craig and Irfan had meetings all day, so I decided to explore a little, and went for my first walk in Dhaka, ending up at the National Mosque of Bangladesh; Baital Muharram. It was a beautiful building, surrounded by large outdoor courtyards and those in turn surrounded by street markets. Prayer caps, clothes, Tasbih beads, prayer mats, hijabs, sugar cane juice, fresh coconuts, plastic toys, shoes, sandals, shalwar kameez; you name it, it was there. I browsed the market and then went inside to pray; it was Dhuhr, the lunchtime prayer and the place was packed. Afterwards, I did my Sunnah prayers, and sat down on the cold marble floor, staring around at the walls, windows and ceiling. It was at this point that a man came up to me and asked; 'business or pleasure?', pointing at my camera. Not wanting to give any personal information away, I replied 'pleasure'. He said he owned a camera shop in the bazaar next door and invited me for tea and cake. I was mildly suspicious of him, but I accepted nonetheless, and followed him into the adjoining shopping centre to his camera stall, which was well kitted out with stock of all kinds of camera-related equipment. We sipped tea and talked about various camera-related topics and it wasn't long before the same question I get asked on every trip arose; how did I become Muslim?. I took my time telling the story and he seemed full of joy to hear it. His name was Dil Mohammed, he was short, carried a well-fed frame, a beard and a lovely smile. He insisted we meet the following day just after Fajr, the morning prayer, for me to join him on his daily walk. I headed back to the hotel through the heaving potholed streets, and met the guys for dinner.

As promised, the next morning just after sunrise, Dil Mohammed came to the FARS hotel, and off we went. It was a little cooler than the day before but still in the early twenties, with a thin haze in the air. We stopped off on our way at what seemed like an old abandoned office block, which turned out to be a Madrassah of sorts, with different kinds of Islamic lectures being given in each room. He was showing me a place where many locals and foreign travellers would come together for islamic debate and learning. I met a brother from South Africa and started talking to him. He had come to study at this school, and was almost finished. His calm and peaceful demeanour was comforting to be near, if that makes sense, and once more I found myself telling him the story of my journey to Islam. Dil Mohammed signalled for us to leave and we said our Salaams and headed out towards the park.

It was a really long walk, but also a very beautiful one in the national gardens. What amazed me was the number of elderly people out at that time of the morning, taking in exercise. The brother asked if I wanted my picture taken, so I posed for one, leaning against a massive tree. Something small bit my hand, enough to sting, but not enough to show a bite mark. I looked closely at the bark of the tree and saw what I can only describe as a tiny red ladybug. We left the park and took a walk around the neighbouring street markets, which were selling all kinds of bright coloured fruit and vegetables and different types of fish. It was here that I started feeling dizzy and woozy, so I thanked Dil Mohammed for showing me around, made my excuses and returned to the hotel. We still keep in touch and we have met up a couple of times since on other trips I have made to Bangladesh.

I slept most of the day until the late afternoon, where we checked out and boarded a flight to Jessore in the South West of Bangladesh. I had never been on a bombardier four hundred twin propeller plane before, and I was nervous at first. What if the engines fail? Aren't these planes dangerous? As the throbbing of the engines and propellers hit a crescendo, and we rolled forward, I was mesmerised at the patterns the spinning blades made, and in minutes we were up in the air, with the sun reflecting off of the myriad of interlinked waterways and ponds below. One chicken burger, slice of cake and a mango juice later, we were in Jessore. We arrived at the hotel and I flaked out, still feeling a little unsteady from the mornings activity. I still don't know to this day what had bitten me.

After an early breakfast, we set off in an air-conditioned minibus for a few hours, until we reached a wide river and could go no further. We piled onto a boat and crossed the 500-metre wide waterway, passing boats coming the other way, carrying motorcycles, people, animals and any thing or anyone that needed to get to the other side. There was the sounds of the chug-chugging of the outboard motor and the swishing, rippling sound of water running along the side of the long wooden boat. A huge container ship passed in front of us and seemed so out of place in this brown watery and palm tree banked environment. Fully in the moment, sun beating down on my face, I took a mental snap of where I was. Definitely better than sitting in an edit suite somewhere in soho!

Waiting for us was Shaikh Madani's brother and a motorised Rickshaw. I had met Shaikh Madani a few weeks earlier whilst filming in Gambia with Penny Appeal. He had come out from the UK along with singer, Harris J. and a few others. Shaikh Madani is a prominent figure in the Bangladeshi community in London, and is a truly beautiful human and a wise scholar, so to meet his father and brother in their own house was an honour. Again, the road ran out and we transferred to motorbikes. On either side of us were fishing pools and streams, boats, nets and bamboo. The sun was now directly above our heads and everything shone, glinted and reflected its blinding rays. The project we were visiting was a madrasah [1] and an orphanage and it was run by Shaikh Madani's father.

I set the camera up and interviewed the Imam, a teacher, and some of the students. The students, whose ages ranged from around eight until eighteen, were all buzzing to see the camera equipment and 'Ghora', or white man in their school. The large building was almost finished, and it was like a monolith rising out of the wetlands. This made filming it difficult, as being unfinished, it looked a bit messy; concrete here and there, building materials scattered around and piles of bricks everywhere. I made the best of a challenging situation and then moved onto the food preparation in the bamboo and palm leaf hut, set just behind the school in the recreational area. Riz had joined us and was talking me through the cooking process of rice, curry and dhal, and then the food being served to the students, which would make a nice little video once edited together. When we had wrapped up the filming, we joined the others in Shaikh Madani's father's house, and hungrily tucked into the array of fresh curries laid out in front of us. To this day, I have never seen king tiger prawns as big as the ones we ate. They were the size of half of my hand at least, and succulent, meaty, clean and fresh having been pulled out of the river less than an hour before. Returning the way we came, we got back to the airport, just in time for the flight back to Dhaka. After the twin propellor plane had landed, we

---

[1]   Religious school

jumped straight in a people carrier and set off northwards towards Netrakona, a remote rural town.

*   *   *

Four hours, countless ridiculous dad jokes and a few hundred miles later, we arrived at our hotel with an escort of six armed policemen. It happened to be the only hotel in Netrokona. And it wasn't pretty. The first room I was shown wasn't too bad, but sadly the presenter and 'talent' Riz had earmarked it for himself so I was relegated to the next available one. Mildew stained walls, mould, damp mattress and curtains. The bed was rock solid. I was horrified, and had never stayed anywhere like this before. The only thing to do once I had given the room a sweep for spiders with my phone torch, was to cover myself head to toe with mosquito repellent, lie like a mummy, fully clothed, hoodie up, strings pulled so only my eyes were showing, sheet over my head and tucked underneath me. Surprisingly I had a very good nights sleep.

The program I was there to film was called 'Open Your Eyes', which was an eyesight and cataract clinic. It was set in the compound of a medical centre, surrounded by rice fields, palm trees and high banks. The courtyard was already full of prospective patients, who would register, get observed and if they needed to, get referred for treatment in Dhaka or be given a prescription for anything treatable on site. By the end of the afternoon, everyone had been seen by the doctors, nurses and opticians and were either heading home after being referred to the Eye hospital in Dhaka, or waiting to hand their prescriptions in to the temporary pharmacy. As the metal gate for the pharmacy slid open there was a mad rush, and only the armed policemen from our escort stopped a stampede. It was absolute mayhem, with people shouting and waving their pieces of paper in the air, and the police having to keep order. Eventually, all the prescriptions were handed out and and calm descended once more. It had been an intensive day of filming, from taking case studies and following them, through the eye check ups, through to diagnosis; and then either referral or being sent to the on-site pharmacy. Hot

47

and humid, our convoy of people carriers and the police escort headed back to the hotel.

I decided to go for a walk when we got back, but I was told by the police captain that I should stay in the hotel as Netrakona wasn't a safe place. But I didn't care at this point. The intensity of the days situation made me want to strike out on my own, as we had been shadowed by, and were under the security of the local police for twenty-four hours a day. I wanted to have a look around, and feel the environment without being shown here, taken there or guarded by anyone. From the interactions I had with people throughout this trip to Bangladesh, I didn't feel in any danger or any hostility. In fact I felt nothing but welcomed by everyone I had met, if not a bit of a curiosity. So I set off into the town alone, taking in the one main street, soaking up the sights and sounds. I stopped to buy a bottle of sprite and saw an island outcrop in the river behind the shops. On there were a dozen or so lads playing football. Asking the shopkeeper how to get there, he pointed for me to walk about 100 yards and then cross over the river. Between two houses, there was an old brick, concrete and scaffolding pole bridge, which crossed over a stretch of water covered in lily pads. It was such a beautiful sight, only spoiled by the rubbish strewn on the banks from the backs of the shops and houses. Vines hung from trees and covered the sides of the bridge, and it was like something from an Indiana Jones movie. There is something really special about going for a wander in a foreign country, not knowing where you are going or where you will end up. I had yet another moment on this bridge... I was in the heart of rural Bangladesh, on my own and living in the moment. Pretty special. This was an adventure and I felt completely in tune with the environment. The boys playing football waved me to come over and join them, and I didn't need asking twice. We had a kick around for a while, them asking me if I liked Chelsea or Manchester United. Obviously the answer was Chelsea, but more importantly, and on every trip I have been on now, I educated them in the ups and downs of being a Bristol Rovers fan.

As the sun started its descent behind the palm trees on the horizon, they invited me to join them for Maghrib, the evening prayer at their mosque, one hundred or so metres away. We walked along narrow paths, under hanging vines and over-hanging trees to the mosque, where the Imam asked me where I was from? I replied England, UK, and told him I was Muslim. He asked me my name. 'Muhammad Mateen' I replied. 'You can't have that name' he retorted. 'It must be Muhammad Abdul Mateen'. As it turns out, the Islamic name I had taken wasn't fully correct, as one is not supposed to have the name of the Prophet Muhammad (peace be upon him) and one of Allah's ninety nine names together. There is supposed to be a name in between, so after sixteen years of being Muhammad Mateen, I became Muhammad Abdul Mateen. The Imam offered me what I consider a great honour; to lead the prayers, but I was very nervous about pronouncing the Arabic prayers I had learned incorrectly, so regrettably I declined and followed his lead instead. This was another very special moment for me and one I hold very dearly. After prayers, we drank tea and ate cake at the Madrassah school, took some photos with the students and then said our farewells.

Finding my way back wasn't so easy, as it was pitch black apart from a few flickering exterior lights on some of the huts and houses. The mosquitos were out en masse and having a fine feast on my blood. At the main road through town, I tried to wave down a motorised Tuk Tuk, but could only find an elderly gentleman on a bicycle Rickshaw. I jumped on, and this man who was lean strong and wiry, cycled me back to the hotel. It was only a few hundred metres, but I thought he was going to expire, the poor guy. The road, if you could call it that was pot holed, pitted, cratered and full of stones and rocks, and certainly put any gripes I may have had about filming that day fully into perspective. Back at the hotel, the police were relieved to see me return in one piece, and laughed at my apparent insanity of wandering off. We all had dinner and this night, I was put into a better room. Irfan came to my room around 11pm for a coffee, cigarette and to see how I thought this part of the trip had gone. By 2.30am, I had learned about his childhood, upbringing, joining the police academy and them moving to Austria and becoming a pilot. Also about the amazing work he has done around the world with many charities and also the UN. I could have listened to him all night and I think Irfan could have talked for longer, but an early start was needed in the morning so we called it a night.

We set off just after Fajr prayer and the weather had turned. There was an immense thunder storm, and the air was thick with electricity. White, purple and blue flashes filled the sky, closely followed by huge cracks and rolls of thunder. As we drove along the main road through the town, it started to pour with torrential rain. We hit the regional border and said goodbye and thank you to our police escort. The captain had an amazing bright orange, henna-dyed beard, and I couldn't resist a selfie with him. All smiles and Salaams, we parted company on to a crazy drive back to Dhaka, our driver playing chicken with cars and trucks. Four hours later we were on the outskirts of Dhaka. Now one might expect the drive from the northern city limits to the centre might take an hour, or two perhaps? No. Five hours to cross half the city. I had never seen such static yet fluid traffic. It sounds like a complete contradiction, but the way I saw it, was like an hourglass and grains of sand. Or quicksand maybe. Every type of vehicle you can imagine was pushing, edging, scraping, honking and beeping their way in the general direction of everywhere and nowhere, all at the same time. Without a doubt, Dhaka was and has been since, the worst traffic I have ever experienced anywhere in the world.

Within twelve hours we were in the air once more and heading home. In the transit point in Dubai, I ran into the South African brother I had met in the Madrassah. We prayed together and parted company once more. Such a nice surprise and round-up to the trip. This had been my introduction to a beautiful country with beautiful people and the first of five trips there to date. And I became Muhammad Abdul Mateen. Beautiful Bangladesh, Alhamdulillah.

6

Myanmar

'Myanmar's Rohingya, a centuries-old Muslim minority group, have been subjected to sharply escalating persecution by the Myanmar army, and by a particular sector of extreme nationalist Buddhist monks.

A brutal attack marking a new level of violence against the Rohingya occurred in 2012 and led to the flight of thousands to other countries. More recently, military forces entered one of the rural areas occupied by the Rohingya. They destroyed at least 1,500 buildings and shot unarmed men, women and children dead. Earlier this week a video emerged showing villagers sitting on the ground with their arms over their heads, as soldiers appear to beat one of the men.'

Source - The Guardian, 04/01/2017

Within six days of returning from Bangladesh, I was on a flight, with Irfan and Riz, to Myanmar. We flew via Bangkok to Yangon and then onto Sittwe, in Rakhine State; a region where many of the Rohingya had had their land taken off them and been corralled into 'villages'. These were not so much villages as concentration camps, as we were to later discover. I had been warned that this trip could be very tricky, due to the violence directed at the Rohingya population, and the tight security of a nation that had been under military rule for decades, until Aung San Suu Kyi became the country's elected leader. The Rohingya are the indigenous Muslim population of Myanmar, who had been persecuted by the non-Muslim majority for generations. It was three months before the outright genocide that killed thousands of people. This time, I was going in undercover as a project officer and not a videographer. I will say that again. I went in UNDERCOVER! Cool or what?! From the moment I heard this in the office in Wakefield, I knew that this would be a different kind of trip. The reason for this was the Myanmar Government, lead by Aung San Suu Kyi was fearful and restrictive of foreign media, especially around the human rights abuses of the Rohingya Muslim minority in Rakhine State, which borders Bangladesh. Even though Aung San Suu Kyi, a Nobel laureate, fought for freedom herself against the military Junta that held her under house arrest for many years, it seemed odd to me that she would allow such brutality and oppression to happen within her own borders. It made me wonder if she, herself was just a puppet or facade for the real power behind the scenes; the Myanmar military generals. [2] If asked, my camera was solely for personal use as I was a 'keen nature and landscape photographer'. Plausible reason for sure. The government were suspicious of every foreigner that visited, especially NGOs and their staff, so I was to just smile, nod and say as little as possible, if or when asked questions about the purpose of the visit.

We flew direct to Bangkok on a thirteen hour flight, then had a rushed transit to fly to Yangon in Myanmar. Surprisingly, I didn't face any questions when we arrived and immigration and passport control was straightforward. From Yangon we flew by yet another twin prop plane to Sittwe. The hotel we stayed in was a palace compared to my experience in Bangladesh the week before; clean white walls, dry bedding, and generally in touch with the 21st century. There were palm trees dotted around the courtyard and a large swimming pool in the centre of it. There were a lot of lizards on the walls, which didn't bother me at all, as spiders were and still are, my heart stopping phobia. We checked in, got changed and walked across the road to the long sandy beach. Irfan and I went for a swim and then joined in some beach football with some of the local guys. It was a stunning place, with the beach being an almost grey-black, the sun reflecting off the pools and ripples and making little rainbow patterns in the wet sand, almost like oil on water. Every chance I

---

2   She has since been deposed by her Generals in a military coup and imprisoned for thirty three years on charges of corruption.

get, on any trip, if I can make it into the sea, a lake or a river, I will have a swim, especially if it's hot. Supper was followed by swapping stories and then the familiar battle of trying to get to sleep in a very different timezone.

It was the second week of May 2017, and was very balmy 39°C at 8am in Sittwe and the humidity was at 100%. We were taken to the ground partners office to meet the staff, then we set off for the Rohingya settlement. I had noticed a car with blacked out windows following us wherever we went. The night before, I had been asked to send some footage of Bangladesh to be shown on a screen in the background of the studio back in the UK, so on our way to the Rohingya enclosure, we had pulled over to get a better signal on the mobile I was using to upload the footage with. The car pulled over too and waited for us. We pulled away and drove for quite some time, then stopped for a cup of tea at a roadside stop. A guy came and sat next to us, dressed in civilian clothes. It turns out he was a secret service officer and was openly watching what we were doing and listening in to our conversation. He literally sat amongst our group and took in the conversation. His English was immaculate and he was very friendly toward us, although he made no attempt to disguise the fact he was there to keep an eye on our every move. It was pretty surreal to be honest.

When we arrived at the first Rohingya village, it seemed to be in the middle of nowhere. The roads we took were dusty, overgrown and winding left and right, between thickets of trees and paddy fields, and obviously a road not taken unless travelling to the village itself. It felt like some kind of self preservation, as remote as possible, hiding out of sight and difficult to get to; i.e. one would not be going there unless they had a reason to go there. We wandered through the village, between bamboo huts and shelters. It had been built on the edge of an old quarry, with huts cropping up all around the rim of the small cliff sides. We talked to a number of families about the homes they were living in, which had been built by the charity. They were sturdy affairs, and assembled by the Rohingya men. One guy who was hammering nails into some wooden support struts, saw me, smiled and waved. His buddy was preparing the beams laid on the ground and was a dead ringer for Brad Pitt. Well I thought so. We communicated though a few words, gestures and smiles, then I took their photos and continued along the dusty road towards the project.

The project was a good one as it empowered the community to build for themselves and give the men a purpose other than sitting around like in other situations I had witnessed in the past. Many of them had lost everything as they had fled abuse and violence in some of the areas they had lived. Here, they were all together and away from trouble and at least they could stick together and build a community. Their lands had been confiscated by the state and they had absolutely nothing, other than items they had managed to hustle for, or had been given. We were shown around the small village, and Riz and I posed for a photo with all the children. When I look at those photos today, what haunts me is I have no idea who survived the unforeseen and imminent genocide, and who was murdered in cold blood, and I will never know.

Under the cover of a tarpaulin, strung up between three trees, was a widow and her three children. They had no shelter from the heat and lived there as if it were their home. It was heartbreaking to see, but there was nothing we could do about it, other than discreetly and secretly give her some money to buy anything she may need until her bamboo home had been built. There is only so much one can do in reality when in the field, but we pushed for her and her children to be housed imminently. Whether this happened I don't know.

On day two, we set off again and once more the car with the blacked-out windows was right behind us. It wasn't until we arrived at the checkpoint to enter the Rohingya area, that they left us alone. This checkpoint was pretty nerve-wracking for me. I had hidden my camera, tripod and sound kit under the seat and covered it with a few items of clothing. It was vital that the checkpoint police didn't find it, or it could have spelled trouble and jeopardised not only the distribution, but also our liberty. This may all sound dramatic, but in all honesty, it's no joke when you are in these environments. Things can be pretty cut and dry in regards to any particular nations' take on journalism, reporting or filming as a form of espionage, and a situation can get out-of-hand in a matter of seconds if precautions aren't taken. Our passport numbers were taken, photos taken and the barbed wire barrier was lifted for us to drive through. On either side of us were 8-10 metre wire fences with razor wire on the top, giving a prison or holding-camp feel. We drove through a long road until the fences widened to surround an area of trees and huts. This is where the Rohingya lived. All of the surrounding land had been theirs, but the government had disenfranchised them and seized it all, corralling them into this two or so kilometre square holding pen. We were told that they weren't allowed to leave the compound apparently for their own safety, but also people weren't allowed in unless given direct permission from the government. There were a few stalls selling basic items here and there, but that was it. Food was scarce and the situation was desperate. We weaved our way through the temporary bamboo structures and came into a clearing in the centre of the village. Here, was a truck unloading boxes of food aid for the villagers. Behind was a 'Feed Our World' banner strung between two palm trees and a number of orange t-shirts, stacking the boxes ready for the distribution. Riz looked at me, very concerned. In each box was a bag of rice and a bottle of oil. That was it! The authorities had only allowed these items to be included in the distribution, and no pulses, beans, sugar, salt or spices. As with most things in this country, we were powerless to do anything about it and could only do as directed by the authorities. Each person was issued a number, and in turn would hand it over and then put a thumb print next to their name and number. This signified that they were then able to queue up to receive the aid. Again, it was a hot and humid day, so I had taken on a lot of water, therefore needing to use some local facilities... One of the ground partner staff told me to jump on the back of his bike, and he took me a few hundred yards to the Mosque, where I was able to use the facilities and then pray. The ride back was hilarious as I decided to film the journey, whipping through the narrow sandy paths and ducking under hanging trees. Making it back safely, I continued filming for the rest of the afternoon. Riz helped one small girl carry her rice and oil back to her home. It was so sad to see them all living in basic conditions and in constant fear of what was going to happen next, especially in light of the authorities removal of their lands and rights, and random but growing physical attacks on them. What made it worse was that there was nothing that we could do about it and it was heartbreaking.

We left the enclosure the same way we came in, and once more I hid the camera equipment under the seats and covered it with clothing. After signing out, I was relieved and grateful to get back to the hotel for a dinner consisting of more than just rice and oil.

Before we left Sittwe, I had backed up all the footage on to separate hard drives. I gave one to Riz, one to Irfan, made a copy on my laptop, hidden under 'Bristol Rovers Project', and stashed the memory cards amongst the clothes in my suitcase. I didn't want to take any chances. Arriving at the airport, I started to feel very nervous. What if I got searched? I had been told that they most probably would pull my bags apart and go through everything with a fine toothed comb. My stomach was starting to summersault after going through security, which turned out to be a typical search and no one asked me to switch on my laptop or see what was on my camera. I decided to talk to the nice lady on the passport and immigration desk, saying to her what a beautiful country Myanmar was, and that I would love to return one day. I also asked her where the bathroom was, as I was feeling unwell due to something I had eaten; being able to carry this off as the nerves had knotted my stomach. Amazingly she didn't ask too many questions, and we all went through to the duty free and departure lounge. It seemed all too easy. An hour later we were sat on the plane taxiing onto the runway. This is where my imagination ran away from me. The engines had started to rev up to head down the runway, when all of a sudden, they stopped. I could see what I thought was a police car heading towards the plane. 'Oh no!' I thought...'They've realised their mistake and they're coming to get me'. Clammy hands and sweat building, my imagination ran wild, and I fast forwarded to me being sat in some dank mouldy cell with spiders mosquitos and bugs. Rotten rice, dirty water and explosive diarrhoea. Snapped back to reality by the engines roaring once more, we started to move. In reality, I think it was only an airport car crossing the runway, but I had been so uptight about getting the footage out, anything slightly out of the norm became thoughts of the government authorities on their way to get me, sort me out, and lock me up!

Once the wheels lifted off of the ground, I finally relaxed. However, my fears proved to be right as I would discover nine months later.

Within three months, tens of thousands of Rohingya Muslims were slaughtered by the military and local Rakhine population. According to an article on the 8th March 2018 in Time Magazine, *'Based on surveys of refugees who fled Myanmar for neighbouring Bangladesh, 28,300 Rohingya children have lost at least one parent, while an additional 7,700 children reported having lost both parents, according to the ASEAN Parliamentarians for Human Rights (APHR), citing data from the Bangladeshi government. That puts the number of "lost" parents as high as 43,700, according to APHR, adding that it is unclear how many of the children are siblings and may have lost the same parent.'* The horrors of what actually happened were shared with me first hand upon my return to Bangladesh in February 2018, and which I shall go into detail in 'Chapter 8 - Rohingya'.

7

Bashir, Boonaa
and Ethiopia

'Contaminated water and poor sanitation are linked to transmission of diseases such as cholera, diarrhoea, dysentery, hepatitis A, typhoid and polio. Absent, inadequate, or inappropriately managed water and sanitation services expose individuals to preventable health risks. This is particularly the case in health care facilities where both patients and staff are placed at additional risk of infection and disease when water, sanitation and hygiene services are lacking. Globally, 15% of patients develop an infection during a hospital stay, with the proportion much greater in low-income countries.

Some 842 000 people are estimated to die each year from diarrhoea as a result of unsafe drinking-water, sanitation and hand hygiene. But diarrhoea is largely preventable, and the deaths of 361 000 children aged under 5 each year could be avoided each year if these risk factors were addressed. Where water is not readily available, people may decide hand washing is not a priority, thereby adding to the likelihood of diarrhea and other diseases.'

Source - WHO

Throwing back to my first day at Penny Appeal in 2017, I had been given a project to work on. It was to make a documentary film about a guy name Bashir Osman. Bashir was an engineering student, who had fled the civil war in Somalia with his parents and siblings in 1992, and had been the President of FOSIS, The Federation of Student Islamic Societies. Not only this, but he had taken on a huge challenge; to raise £165,000 and build 50 water wells in East Africa; 40 in Somalia and 10 in Ethiopia. In 2015, he had been on a lecture tour in Switzerland. It had been a hot day during the holy month of Ramadan, and Bashir decided to take a swim to cool down in a river but tragically, he drowned. He was only 26 when he passed away, and it was a huge blow for everyone who knew or came into contact with him. It was a terrible and traumatic loss for his family. Wanting to fulfil his dream, Bashir's family and friends took up the mantle, and continued to fundraise in his memory, until the target had been beaten; a whopping great £169,000. Amazingly, in the autumn of 2014, I had been attending a business conference in Rotterdam, with my good friend and entrepreneur Humraz Khan, where we were introduced to Bashir in the foyer of the building. Such a small world and an amazing coincidence.

Three months had passed since I had been given the project, and I had come up with nothing. This was partly due to the intense workload and travelling involved with the job, but also part procrastination. It wasn't going to be an easy thing to do, down to the sensitivities involved with a project such as this, plus I had been given no guidance, just told to 'get on with it'. It wasn't until I had been filming a video with Boonaa Mohammed, a Canadian-Ethiopian film director, writer and poet, that everything fell into place. Boonaa and Bashir had been friends and when I mentioned that I might go to Ethiopia to film a few of his wells and the communities they had benefitted, Boonaa agreed to come on board. Plans were quickly drawn up, budgets made, schedules drawn out and the ground partner contacted. I had always just turned up and done my thing on every mission so far.. point a camera and shoot. Everything else was taken care of by someone else. This was the first time I had been responsible for absolutely everything on a trip. Hello imposter syndrome! Once more the self doubt and fear reared its ugly head. However this time, I managed to to get a handle on it. This was now my eighth field mission and I was fully in charge. The responsibility and buck stopped with me, but I felt I was ready for this now. I hadn't messed up on any of my previous trips and had managed to deliver everything that was asked of me. I knew what I wanted to film and how to film it. Now it was just a case of meticulously planning the trip from top to bottom.

Once Boonaa had flown in from Canada, I picked him up from Heathrow airport and we drove to Birmingham. There we interviewed Faizal Malik, a friend of Bashir's from University and then vice-president of FOSIS, and then drove over to Bashir's house. Here we met his mother Murayo and two of his brothers, Ayaanle and Zakariye. It had been two years since the passing of Bashir, and his death was understandably still very raw for his family. They had tentatively agreed to the documentary, but I felt it necessary to speak with them in person, and be completely transparent with the aims of the film. It would celebrate the life of Bashir, and also be used to inspire more people to continue his legacy of building wells, and his ultimate dream of engineering projects to help improve the infrastructure in East Africa. After a couple of hours of conversation around the film, and my promise to not release anything until they had viewed it first, the family agreed to let me proceed with it. This meant so much to me, to gain their trust with such a delicate, personal and painful area of their lives.

Boonaa and I left their house, with a view to drive to Leicester to meet Bashir's sister Abyaan, and it was at this moment that a call came through from Head Office, saying that there was civil unrest in Awassa, the region in Ethiopia where Bashir's wells were situated. The ground partner had insisted that the situation on the ground was too volatile and not safe to visit. This came less than 24 hours before our departure, so all flights had been booked and I was told that it was my call whether to go ahead, or to scrap the documentary and cut the losses already incurred. We had just promised Bashir's family that we would make a strong film in his memory, and I felt it would have been insensitive, wholly inappropriate and unkind to have put them through the meeting we just had and then suddenly backtrack. Boonaa and I looked at what options we had to film in Addis Ababa, plus the option for us to fly to Harar in the east of the country, where his family came from, to look at possible water related projects. There was also the slight possibility of the situation in Awassa calming down. I made the decision to go ahead.

* * *

After our meeting with Bashir's sister Abyaan, we headed back to London, handed the rental car in and landed in Addis Ababa twelve hours later. I didn't know what to expect from Ethiopian Airlines, but I was very impressed. Plenty of legroom, great food, and some funky bass jazz music piping through the speakers. It was a direct flight to Addis Ababa and once we had landed, we passed through immigration at a snail's pace. Exiting the airport, we headed to the north of the city, where we spent the first four days of the trip, which were a real eye opener. There were piles of human excrement along the side of the roads, rubbish everywhere and it was heaving with people. The hotel was really nice thankfully, and Boonaa introduced me to the local dish of tibs and injera, meat with a sourdough pancake. This was our staple for the rest of the trip.

On our first day, we attended Jummah at a mosque near the centre of the city. The drive there was hectic, as we had jumped into one of the many blue Lada taxis that were zipping around the streets. Driving through the city, we saw the old presidential palace where former Marxist Dictator Mengistu had directed his militia to carry out political arrests and murders during the late 1970's and 1980's. This of course, was one of the causing factors behind the 1984 famine and resulting deaths countrywide. We passed markets, the football stadium and a rubbish tip on the way to the mosque. There were animals roaming around everywhere, and the cows and goats were eating anything they could find, which was rather disturbing when I saw a cow munching on a blue plastic bag.

The mosque was situated off the main road and had a huge courtyard with trees and surrounding buildings. I filmed Boonaa walking across the courtyard and into the mosque itself, where we did our ablutions and sat down on the floor. Just before the Khutbah, which is the sermon before the prayer, there was a commotion in the front row. We watched as an elderly man was lifted up carried out of the prayer hall. Apparently he had passed away. The khutbah was given, Jummah prayers were prayed and Janazah (funeral) prayers were said for the man. It occurred to me, that as a Muslim, it wasn't a bad way to go.

We filmed a few experimental videos, one in particular for Boonaa's poem 'Mercy'. This worked out well, but we decided that there wasn't much point in staying in the capital any longer, so we booked flights to Dire Dawa, from where we would go on to Boonaa's family in Harar. In the afternoon we headed down to the national stadium for a wander around the leather shops. I picked up a soft brown leather bomber jacket, which has accompanied me on every trip since. It was a bustling hive of activity; families out for an afternoon walk, bartering with stall holders and shopkeepers for gifts, clothes and toys. It had been raining for most of our time there, so everyone seemed to be taking advantage of a break in the bad weather. Stopping off for a coffee, Boonaa spied a food stall and ordered some tibs and injera. Wherever I travel, I never eat street food and am very careful to not eat salads or have ice cubes when in a hotel, because of the water that the cubes are made from, and the salad is generally washed in tap water. The lamb, from which the meat was being cut, was covered in flies and very unappealing. As the food was brought out, Boonaa offered me some and I politely declined, explaining my street food rule. He asked me if I trusted him and I replied 'of course'. 'Say bismillah and take some then brother, you'll be fine!'. I broke my rule.

As we boarded the twin propeller bombardier plane, we came face-to-face with the heads of the Ethiopian Orthodox Church. Everyone embarking the flight asked for a blessing, pilots included. One of the bishops asked where I was from and I explained why we were in Ethiopia. We spoke for a little while, then the seatbelt signs came on and the plane taxied onto the runway. Just as the propellers were at full speed and the wheels lifted off the tarmac, I felt my stomach do a 360 degree turn. Then again. A stabbing pain in my gut became so intense, I realised that I had to take action, so unbuckled my seatbelt, jumped out of the seat and pulled myself up the headrests towards the toilet at the front of the plane. It was still climbing so the flight attendant told me to sit down, but I knew what I had to do. I jumped into the toilet, locked the door and only re-emerged 45 mins later as we were coming in to land. I had been so sick, and I pity everyone on that flight if you get what I mean.

By the time Boonaa's cousin Yahya came to pick us up, I was feeling much better. The drive to Harar was a beautiful route, through hills and valleys, and within an hour or so, we were pulling into a hotel at the gates of the city. Harar is widely called the fourth Medina. It was the place where the Prophet Mohammed (peace be upon him) and his family stayed in exile. There is a wall surrounding the city and there are 99 mosques inside; one for every three houses. Narrow dust and stone alleyways wind between the ancient houses, up and down the hillside. We went for a walk around the perimeter and people were calling out 'Ferenge'.. which means foreigner. Many of the Muslim population of Ethiopia are of the Oromo tribe, as are Boonaa's family. In Yahya's house, his wife picked some fresh coffee beans, rand roasted them. It was captivating to see this organic process from start to finish, through a smoky blue atmosphere. She then ground them and served us 'Bunna' coffee. Very strong and fruity flavoured. I was even given the Oromo name 'Ibsa', which is like 'John' or 'Dave' in English. We spent the evening talking of our plans to film any water-related content that we could find, and then retired to our hotel.

It was a very restless sleep, and the next morning we set out to a dried-up lake, where farmers were having to dig pits in the lake bed to hit the already sinking water table. This is where they would get the water for their animals, but not themselves, as a water pipeline had recently been installed, thus giving the residents a new clean source of water. I managed to get some great footage of these water pits and interviewed a local farmer, but there was nothing that we could use for Bashir's documentary. Wondering if I had made a terrible mistake on going ahead with the trip, I later spoke with Boonaa who agreed to come back for a second trip to Awassa and would donate his time. This made me feel a whole lot better, even thought we had filmed some good content for other projects related to Boonaa and the charity.

That evening, we drove down to a slaughterhouse on the edge of the city, where wild hyenas would come to feed off the discarded scraps of meat. I had seen online before we left the UK, that this had become a tourist attraction, by people feeding these wild beasts themselves, whether by hand or on a stick protruding from their mouths. I had a go myself, and was going to try feeding from the mouth, however the guy cutting the meat on the stick couldn't remember which end had been given to the last hyena, so I settled for feeding by hand instead. I'm glad I did, because hyenas are scary looking animals with big teeth, and I didn't fancy having my face chewed off accidentally. These prehistoric creatures would make a whooping, laughing sound, the hair on their necks bristling and their intelligent beady eyes sizing up the onlookers around them. Kneeling in the dust, illuminated by car headlights, I held my hand out and pointed the meat-covered stick towards an expectant hyena. It prowled forward and took the meat in one swift movement, turned and moved back into the darkness. Seeing it up-close was amazing, although very brief. I stood up and made way for the next person. As we got back in the car, I could see a mass of shadows and reflecting eyes moving around the vicinity. There must have been a dozen at least, and it crossed my mind, that if they got annoyed or decided to try something a little bigger for dinner, we would have been in trouble. Thankfully, they were satisfied with the current menu.

I think that this was the first trip where I used poetry to try to process the whole experience, probably in ways only I could understand. I had started to write abstract words and lines down, and never completed a poem as such at the time. Eighteen months later, I managed to pull my chaotic threads into a coherent form:

Harar

High walls open as we move slowly
Following 70's benz with a back seat of modesty
Steep roads filled with the first sight
Of everyday orderly chaos
Plastered walls wind up and down
To our home for the coming hours.

Sitting, slowly roasting beans freshly picked
She moves them from green to brown
From pot to cup to mouth
With blue smoke and green shoots
Ingest, inhale, imbibe
Ibsa, Oromo, immersed.

Tracing the walls circling 99 masjids
Past the hyenas feeding on selfies
This ferengé, a curious suspicion
Weaving through grinning handshakes
And red eyed stares
Breathes in this 4th Medina.

Power cut candles flickering
The Maghreb group gathered in lines
To turn will and give thanks
Ask forgiveness and guidance
Hearts within walls inside walls
More open than the plains.

Matt Robinson, Jan 2019

Ethiopia made a huge impression on me and was now engraved into my heart. I couldn't wait to get back.

*   *   *

Six weeks later, and after much planning, Boonaa returned to the UK and we set off for Ethiopia once more. The situation in Awassa had calmed down and our ground partner, Mohammed Ibrahim had made all the arrangements for us to get out into the remote hills where the water wells had been installed. Rather than fly to Awassa, he had decided to send a driver to pick us up instead. The drive was supposed to take five hours, but like most road trips on these missions, it took almost twice that time. The road was basically made of gravel, which would kick up a lot of dust from anything travelling along it. This is how the road system worked in Ethiopia; on the outside you'd have people and animals walking, being overtaken by mules and carts, being overtaken by Tuk Tuks, being overtaken by buses and trucks and sometimes cars. In between all this would be motorcyclists, weaving their way through haphazardly and often blind because of the dust. Trucks and buses are kings of the road and within 5 minutes of getting into this journey, we must have had ten near misses. Trucks on the wrong side of the road, appearing out of nowhere from the dust cloud, just in time for our land cruiser to swerve or brake. This kept on happening and after a while, it became an amusement, as each time we laughed at the near misses. I hastily called the UK and requested a flight back for the return journey, so as to not have to run the gauntlet again on this insanely dangerous road.

Awassa is a beautiful lakeside town, two hundred and eighty kilometres by road south from Addis Ababa. The land is lush with greenery everywhere, and red earth at the sides of the road. As we jumped out of the car at the hotel, the courtyard and road was full of Grivet monkeys, a primate native to Ethiopia, Sudan, Djibouti and Eritreya. All very inquisitive and not afraid of humans. I had never been up close to a monkey before and I was a little cautious, as my head told me that they can carry rabies, and all it would take was a scratch or little nip. Ironic as I had been face-to-face with a hyena only six weeks earlier.

We checked in and sat down to eat in the restaurant. Boonaa ordered tibs and injera once more, but I was growing weary of this dish, so ordered fried chicken. Boonaa laughed and said he didn't think it would be a good idea, and this became apparent when it arrived. Burnt a very dark brown, the batter looked unappealing, but I was hungry, so took a bite. Blood poured out of the drumstick, and I dropped it onto the plate in horror. Boonaa laughed in a 'I told you so' kind of way, and I went to bed without eating dinner. The whole experience had killed my appetite.

I was woken early the next morning by the sound of monkeys jumping onto, and running across the tin roofs of an outbuilding in the hotel complex. They really had the run of the place. I ate a breakfast of fruit and oats, then jumped into the land cruiser.

The water wells were situated in the highlands and hills four hours west of Awassa. I was getting used to these long road journeys now, and the countryside was stunning, providing me with plenty of material to film. After what seemed like an age of driving up winding hills, we pulled over to the side of the road and followed Ibrahim into the forest. Boonaa did his presenting to camera and we then attempted to follow in the footsteps of our ground partner Ibrahim, down a steep red earth track. This wasn't easy and I found myself on my backside a couple of times. Boonaa made it down without a slip, and we found ourselves in the bottom of a steep gulley, lush green vegetation and trees around us and the sound of a babbling brook. The brook was actually the main source for a few wells in the area. The spring source had been capped off with concrete, and pipelines then ran down and across the hills in different directions, taking water to the villages. There was an outlet pipe for water at the source, where women and children were filling up their water canisters and taking them home. Mohammed Ibrahim explained that before this well had been installed, locals would have to walk up to six kilometres to another polluted water source, and were suffering from diarrhoea, trachoma and other water borne diseases. This well had changed their lives immeasurably. What struck me, was the fact that the people were there going about their everyday business of collecting clean water. An old lady and young girl emerged from the temperate undergrowth and rainforest, walked up to the spring and filled their canisters. Nothing here was choreographed, it all unfolded naturally before us, and once they had filled their canisters, more people arrived from a different direction. It was a pretty special moment, seeing the immediate difference Bashirs well was making on these locals lives.

Our final stop was in the heart of a village, nestling on a hillside with the most spectacular views. In front of us the terrain stretched out in undulating hills and mountains as far as the eye could see. As the jeep pulled up, we could see many villagers in the vicinity of the well. Children running around, one rolling an old bicycle tyre with a stick, some playing tag, and women and girls carrying bags and bundles of clothes to wash. The well itself was a terracotta-coloured concrete structure, with taps on either side. This made it far easier to use for mothers carrying children, as no pumping was needed, and even smaller children could operate the taps. A few metres away on either side were washing tables and sinks, built to wash clothes and also for hygienic purposes. I asked to interview one of the elders of the village, and he agreed. Our only problem was that we needed a three-way translation. Mohammed Ibrahim didn't understand the dialect of this guy, so another man had to translate to basic Amharic and then to English. The village elder pointed to a place across the other side of the valley, around five kilometres away and said that was where they would have to walk to get water before the well was installed. Boonaa then relayed a very important message to him, telling him Bashir's story and how he had passed away, and his family and friends had raised the money for this and other wells. The elder replied that the well had alleviated their problem with water and all the villagers were eternally grateful and may Allah bless him and his families souls. It was quite an emotional moment for all of us, and the children of the village got together and thanked Bashir one-by-one for the camera. We said our goodbyes, and were chased for a few hundred metres by waving, smiling children. We stopped off for lunch at a restaurant high-up in the mountains, and whilst having another coffee and cigarette, sat on a veranda with the rolling hills and mountains, greenery, red earth and monumental clouds in front of me, I had another moment, realising how lucky I had been to experience the events of the day. I had been filming in the remote mountains of Ethiopia and the red earth on my knees and backside were testimony to that. It's impossible to put into words really.

Mohammed Ibrahim came back to Addis Ababa with us and made sure we had everything we needed. He had booked us into a hotel near the airport for our early morning flight the next day. It happened to be Ethiopian New Year and the whole country was celebrating. In Ethiopia, there are thirteen months and the year 2017 was actually 2008 in their calendars. All very confusing, and I would like to go into it further, but I'm sure google can do a better job of it than me. The streets were full and Boonaa and I went for a walk. This part of town was very clean and we didn't have to watch every step, which was a relief. The atmosphere was very light-hearted and everyone was having fun, so we walked around for a couple of hours, then called it a night. For me, the hardest part of everything we had done so far, was yet to happen.

*   *   *

Upon landing in the UK, we hired a car and drove straight to Birmingham. Boonaa and I stayed in an AirBnB, where we recovered from our flight, and I stayed up and edited a short film, with a couple of highlights of the trip, with the children saying 'Thank you Bashir'. Bashir's family were happy to see us, asking how the trip went. I set up for the interviews in the front room and they all went very well. His mother and brothers talking freely about Bashir, his accident and the legacy since his death. After the interviews, I played the short video I had edited and set up the camera to film his families reactions. It was a very sensitive and emotional moment, and their reactions spoke volumes. It meant so much to them to see the messages of thanks from the very people Bashir had endeavoured to help. It was as if they were seeing his legacy go full circle. Just as we were about to leave, Bashir's mother, Murayo, brought out what I can only call the feast of a lifetime. She had cooked numerous dishes for Boonaa and I, and we sat with Ayaanle and Zakariye and ate melt in the mouth beef, chicken, curries, rice, salads, and of course the mandatory banana. I needed an espresso to stay awake on the drive back to our hotel.

Boonaa and I said our goodbyes at Heathrow and I knew I had a brother for life. After I had interviewed Abyaan in the autumn, I had promised her, Murayo, Zakariye and Ayaanle that I would let them view the film first and make any changes if they wanted. It got the seal of approval and the documentary was finally released in September 2018. Sharing this journey together, and to be welcomed and supported by Bashir's family was something very special, and it felt like a privilege and honour to be involved. The hardest part of all of this project was making sure that I had represented Bashir well, and that it was clear to the viewer, how much of an impact his wells had on the people we met in Ethiopia. In fact it is much bigger than was represented in our documentary film. Bashir's legacy of life lives on and has helped, and continues to help, tens of thousands of people in East Africa. Another life lesson was driven home. Water is life and we in the west take for granted that we can turn a tap and clean fresh drinking water comes out. Millions of people don't have this luxury.

8

The Rohingya

'*Soon after the brutal military campaign against the Rohingya started, Human Rights Watch reported that at least 200 Rohingya villages were destroyed and burned by the military, and an estimated 13,000 Rohingya were killed. Today, more than 890,000 Rohingya refugees are sheltering in Bangladesh's Cox's Bazar region: the biggest cluster of refugee camps in the world. Some 92,000 Rohingya refugees reside in Thailand, 21,000 in India, and 102,000 in Malaysia. The Rohingya also make up a portion of Myanmar's 576,000 internally displaced persons (IDPs).*'

Source - Al Jazeera / HRW

TRIGGER WARNING Before you read this chapter, please be warned that it contains a horrifying first hand account of murder and rape.

*   *   *

It was January 2018 and it had been eight months since my trip to the Rohingya villages in Myanmar. In that time, I had been to Ethiopia twice, and on an emergency response to eastern Iraq in the aftermath of an earthquake. Between the two trips to Ethiopia, there had been a heinous act of genocide carried out on the Rohingya people in Rakhine state, Myanmar. The atrocities were unspeakable, and it is estimated that up to 43,000 people had been murdered by soldiers and marauding local militias and civilians. In the eight months after the genocide, around 900,000 Rohingyas had run for their lives, fleeing across the border into Bangladesh, setting up refugee camps on the steep sloped hills of Teknaf region.

We had landed in Dhaka and flown straight to Cox's Bazaar in the far south eastern corner of the country. It boasted the worlds longest sandy beach at 60 kilometres length. It also was now one of the busiest places in terms of relief in the world, with every charity and NGO you could imagine working there. All under the umbrella and supervision of the ICRC (International Charter of the Red Cross). It was a bigger team from Penny Appeal this time, consisting of Faz, whom I had been with in Iraq in the previous December, Irfan, Riz and Taksima, one of the fundraiser and volunteer co-ordinators from London. The hotel lobby was a hive of activity, with NGO's from all around the world; Japan, Brazil, Turkey, France, UK, USA just to name a few. We checked in and then all convened for dinner in the hotel restaurant. Our ground partner Helal from the charity Aggrajattiya had come to join us, and we spoke until late, discussing the days ahead and what to expect. After dinner, I got talking with a guy called Stu, who was heading up the logistical security with the ICRC for the all of the Rohingya refugee camps. He was a policeman from Australia, a top bloke, and had asked for this sabbatical to be able to use his skills and make a difference to this dire situation. It was a reasonably new posting for him and he was a few weeks into a six-month stint, and missing his family terribly. We connected and surprisingly shared an appreciation of UK Hip Hop, which we found out through him checking my website out. Roots Manuva, Blak Twang, Ty, Skinnyman, Rodney P and my brother from another mother, Joe 'DJ Skitz' Cole. Stu was a huge fan of the scene. Hip Hop, especially UK Hip Hop had been my passion for fifteen years, and to a certain extent, still is today. I had made numerous music videos and been filming a documentary with documentary producer and good friend Malcolm Boyle since 2001, but after 2011, it had been left, untouched in a box in storage. Hip Hop had been replaced by the work I do now, and as much as I love the music, for me, it doesn't come close to this.

At 8am we left the hotel and headed to Balukhali Refugee camp. The drive there was stunning, as we took in the Bay of Bengal on our right, with palm trees and colourful fishing boats bulled up onto the sand and on our left were rice fields and distant undulating tree covered hills. There had been a diphtheria outbreak in this particular camp so were were advised to wear face masks as we entered. It had been four months since the genocide had started and this camp was one of the biggest. A funeral procession passed us as we entered the central area of the camp, and it suddenly reminded us of the stark reality of how harsh life in the camps really was. We looked at the shelters being built by Penny Appeal, the washing and toilet facilities being installed and the general terrain of the camp. This camp just went on and on, covering hillsides for as far as the eye could see. Row upon row of huts and shelters. A refugee camp of a staggering size. It had been a long, dusty hot and sunny day and we were exhausted by the time we returned to the hotel.

On the second day, we drove out to Zero Point, which is on the Naf River, a natural border between Bangladesh and Myanmar. A walk through some rice fields brought us through a clearing in some trees to a small hut and a river bank. In the middle of the river was an island which is accessible via a small footbridge during low tide. On this island were rows of temporary huts, put up by Rohingya refugees. It is classed as no mans land so outside the jurisdiction of Myanmar, but also international law. Beyond that on the other side of the river, around two hundred metres away, were some tree covered hills with a dirt track running along the bottom of them. This was Myanmar. I was filming when I saw a flare shoot up from the Myanmar side of the border. Riz came up to me and told me to step away from the river bank and ideally out of vision. He had been informed by one of the Bangladeshi intelligence officers that we had been spotted by a Myanmar military observer who had sent up the flare to get identification from their own intelligence officers. We could see the sniper and machine gun positions nestled into the hillsides two hundred meters away. It was a genuinely hairy moment. The officer also told Riz that him, Irfan and I would be on a list of security risks for Myanmar, as we had made the film of the state the Rohingya were living in prior to the genocide. We were advised to leave the vicinity and move on, which we did. The list wasn't for a nice cup of tea and a chat either. I don't think I will ever visit Myanmar again, and I never want to. We continued into the camps and filmed a women's safe space and some refugee case studies for the rest of the day.

*   *   *

What I am about to write of next, needs a trigger warning. This was an encounter that lead to me having six weeks of counselling upon my return to the UK. It was truly one of the most upsetting and traumatising experiences of my life and still haunts me to this day.

The days unfolded one-by-one, visiting water wells, play centres and small schools, ante-natal clinics and psychological support centres for women who had faced violence and sexual violence at the hands of the Myanmar military and the civilian militias. It was a lot to take in and the stories were absolutely harrowing. Everyone we spoke to in any number of the camps had the same or similar stories. Family members beaten, raped or murdered. Orphaned children living with relatives or family friends. One support worker for a partner charity was telling us a story of a fifteen year old girl, who had seen her family massacred in front of her. She had been raped, but managed to escape. She hid in a ditch and watched as her sisters and mother tried to run away, but were all shot in the back and killed. For days she wandered, semi-naked, through marshlands and swamps until she managed to cross the border into Bangladesh, and the safety of the camps. Hers was not an unusual story and knowing that almost one million people had to flee such treatment, still leaves me cold.

I think it was in Ukhia refugee camp, although by this time, we had been going back and forth between a few of the camps in the course of a few days, so it's all a bit of a blur in regards to exact location. Our aim for the day was to film a case study of someone who was willing to talk first-hand of their experiences at the hands of the army and civilian militia in Myanmar. We had walked up a long steep dusty track, surrounded by children, laughing and shouting in response to Faz, who was like a pied piper to them. He would say a word, and they would repeat it back. Everyone was having fun and it must have been a welcome and entertaining break from the norms of camp life.

By this time it was the middle of the day and the sun was at its zenith, beating down unforgiving rays and heating the camp to almost 40°C. A red dust was being kicked up in the air by the mass of children running and laughing with Faz, and the air was close with the humidity. I was soaked with the sweat that was pouring off me, and making my eyes sting. Our ground partner ushered us into a small hut, with bamboo and tarpaulin sides and a tin roof. Having to bend down to fit inside, we were greeted by a woman in her twenties and her six year old daughter. It was a complete contrast from the bright outdoors and also a welcome shelter from the heat of the direct sunlight. Riz and I said our Salaams and the translator introduced us. The woman and her daughter had been there for four months, after crossing the border with thousands of other refugees under the cover of darkness. I set up the camera and rode mic, started rolling, and she started to speak…

She had lived with her husband, two sons and daughter in a village in Rakhine state, just across the border from Bangladesh. They had been at home when the soldiers and militia came to their village. The soldiers were pulling men out of the houses and shooting them. First of all they shot and killed her husband and eldest son, right in front of them. This was very hard for her to tell, with her voice wavering and tears starting to roll down her face. We waited in silence until she had composed herself and she continued with her story. Removing her hijab, she showed us the top of her head. It was covered with freshly healed angry red scars. She continued to talk… The scars came from the rifle butts of the soldiers, as they battered her head as she had tried to save her four year old son. They had held him down on the floor and strangled him in front of her and her daughter. She had pleaded with them, then physically tried to pull them off of him, but she wasn't strong enough. Her daughter had been sat with us throughout, listening to her mother talk as if it were a bedtime story, just like any other six year old child would. Angelic faced, looking around, picking her nose, looking at her mother, looking at us. Her expression was blank. A wall behind her eyes. Her mother then showed us similar scars on her daughters head, except some of these were still raw and unhealed. She had got these from trying to stop the soldiers from gang raping her mother, a futile attempt that left them both bloody and battered. The rolling tears turned to sobs, and uncontrollable shaking. Guttural, heart wrenching sobs and groans. I had never heard such a noise nor witnessed so much unfathomable pain in my life. I was struggling with my feelings soon after she had started telling us the living horror they had been through, but now I was biting my lip hard to try to retain composure. I looked at Riz and he was crying. I lost control and started to cry myself. I wanted to say something, or put my hand on her shoulder, but what could I say or do? Nothing anyone could say would make it better. All the while, outside the hut, we could hear Faz and the children playing their game, oblivious to the horrors that had just been related to us. We sat there for what seemed like a few minutes as the mother sobbed uncontrollably, having relived the experience once more. The daughter just sat staring into space. Riz and I composed ourselves. He spoke some words of comfort to her and we both thanked her. For what I couldn't say, and upon reflection, this was the only time on any trip I had filmed, where I felt that we possibly caused more pain and suffering, rather than alleviating it. The mother's intention, and ours, was to let the world know what had happened, and this was probably her only opportunity. Doing good by sharing someones traumatic story, and causing harm to those one is sworn to help really can be a very fine line indeed, and on this day, I couldn't find it.

Riz ensured that she would get everything her and her daughter needed, or that was available in the environment they were in. We said our goodbyes and rejoined the throng of children, red eyed and in a daze. Faz asked me what had gone down in the interview, and I told him everything. He could see the look in both mine and Riz's face and he and Taksima too were hit hard by this. The rest of the day, I walked around filming, but I wasn't really there at all. I just couldn't stop hearing the woman's sobbing and pain. It's really difficult to explain, but seeing another human in such abject pain is so hard, especially when there is nothing that can be done about it. Completely powerless. I sat down on the top of one of the hills with huts sprawling away from us, and asked Taksima a few questions on camera. She had returned to her motherland to help highlight the Rohingyas plight and to experience first hand what the living conditions were and hear the horrors that had befallen them. It was so much for everyone to take in and she too was overcome by emotion. She managed to compose herself and then talked of her experiences. It had been a really tough morning for us all.

*   *   *

Our afternoon was spent filming a clinic and ambulance in the camp, which would assess sick patients then ferry them to hospital as and when needed. I was following Faz talking to patients, doctors and nurses. I could see that he wasn't himself too, and that the week's events in the camps, and what he had seen and heard was taking its toll. We jumped in the ambulance, and accompanied the patient he had been talking to as it headed towards the hospital. After ten minutes of bumping all over the road, dodging trucks, cars, buses and bikes with dust kicking up everywhere, we arrived at the hospital.

We pulled up along the side entrance and two orderlies came out with a wheelchair and stretcher. The hospital had doctors from a French charity seeing to the patients as they arrived, but one of them was unhappy about me filming. She ordered me to walk to the gate where we had driven in through, for health and safety reasons. Obviously I obliged and started filming from a distance. This was when a senior doctor came out, who happened to be English. She told me I couldn't film there, without giving a reason, so I remonstrated, explaining that I needed the footage for fund-raising purposes so that the charity could provide more ambulances. She wasn't having it. Faz then asked her what her problem was, then said 'we are on the same effing side' or something to that effect. Her face froze and she turned to me and asked for the country manager of the charity we were working for. I said to Faz to head back to the car, and gently explained to the doctor that this was his first experience of a refugee camp, and was feeling traumatised from the stories he had been told. I apologised on his behalf and asked her if she could look beyond the issue this once. She nodded, said ok, she understood, then walked off. (Not too long after arriving back in the UK, the abusive conduct of the 'Cameraman' was reported to her superiors and I got hauled over the coals at HQ in Wakefield. Thankfully, my line manager believed me and no disciplinary action was taken.)

It wasn't until we were sat in the air-conditioned minibus, heading back to our hotel, with music playing on the stereo, taking pictures and doing instagram stories of palm trees and sun flares, that it hit me like a ton of bricks. Why were they still there, in that hut on the top of a hill, sat in their memories and pain, having just given me what I wanted on film. The perfect case study. In the can. Hard hitting true story. We had got what we needed and were now laughing all the way back to comfort and peaceful sleep. How could I leave them there? How could I switch so quickly, from shedding tears with them, to having a laugh in a minibus? It just didn't compute. unfathomable. I just felt guilt and a sense of panic so extreme. I froze and felt sick.

The feelings of guilt were something I carried for just over a year until I pushed myself to write this poem about it:

Normalisation

Around 34°C, in an oven like shelter,
Somewhere on the top of a hill
Amongst row upon row of makeshift homes
She sits and tells us
How it happened
When she shows the scars on her head
And the head of her 6 year old daughter
Hers from fighting
Unknown men choking the life from her infant son
Her daughters from fighting
Killers violating a 6 year olds Mother

The sobbing in pain from re-telling and re-living
Animalistic. primitive. Gut wrenching
Vomit inducing pain
There is nowhere to go, but. Sit in it
Re-live.

When on the way back to comfort
Air conditioned
Job done, case study in the can
50 Cent filling our ears
Passing palm trees on insta story
It smacks like a ton of bricks
Hits the heart, taking the breath away.
Why is she there and I here?
How can I leave them there?
How can I switch so quickly
From shedding tears with her
With them
To this
Frivolity. Shallow happiness
Enjoying privilege and freedom
To walk away unscathed.

It's been a year
Since our moment in time
Where she shared her incomprehensible horror
Through shaking sobs
As her little girl sat looking around
Angelic face and picking her nose as any 6 year old should
Where they are now I don't know
Same tent, same hill
In my mind they will always be there
Mother and daughter existing with the dead.

12/04/2019

However it seems that I didn't walk away unscathed. Far from it in fact. Six weeks of trauma counselling upon my return to the UK helped, which was provided through Penny Appeal. But it wasn't until I wrote 'Normalisation', that I managed to 'lay it to rest'. Saying that, even now when I recant this story, I choke up and the tears come. Maybe it's something I will never get over. I spoke to a good friend of mine, Stephen Maud of Cloud9 media, who had been making films for sport relief in Africa. The way he dealt with keeping the people he met, and their stories separate, was to compartmentalise. Tell yourself that this happened before you got there, you are the person's mouthpiece to the world to help improve theirs and others situations, and that their problems are not your responsibility. You are a passing moment in their story and they in yours. Hard to stick to, but very wise words.

But yes, where they are now I don't know. Same tent, same hill. In my mind they will always be there. Mother and daughter existing with the dead.

9

Lebanon

'The Government of Lebanon (GoL) estimates that the country hosts 1.5 million Syrian refugees who have fled their country's conflict since 2011 (including nearly one million registered with UNHCR as of end of September 2018). The Syrian refugee population in Lebanon remains the largest concentration of refugees per capita and the fourth largest refugee population in the world.'

Source - World Food Programme

A prolonged and bloody civil war had decimated Lebanon for fifteen years, from 1975 to 1990, and the capital city Beirut had been at the centre of it. For the years after the collapse of the Ottoman Empire, Lebanon had been under French control until 1943, when it claimed independence. The country consists mainly of four groups; The Maronite Christians and the Sunni Muslims, who mainly populate the coastal towns and north, the Shia Muslims in the south and east and the Druze in the mountainous areas. Lebanon had suffered horrendously for years, with an estimated 120,000 fatalities, and over 1 million people forcibly displaced to its neighbours. These neighbours also got involved, with Syria invading from the north and east, and Israel from the south, occupying Beirut. With the Nakba (catastrophe) happening in Palestine in 1948, there had also been an influx of around 400,000 Palestinians, and in Beirut itself, with populations of approximately 10,000 people were the two Palestinian refugee camps; Sabra and Shatila. In 1982 the IDF (Israeli Defence Force) troops 'guarding' the camps under the command of an officer named Ariel Sharon, stood back and allowed

Christian Phylangist militia to enter the camp and massacre 3,500 Palestinian men, women and children. The camps are still there today with as many as 20,000 people living in cramped conditions.

French and American military barracks blown up, with hundreds of deaths, bombs being dropped by the USA and Israel, it didn't seem the safest place to go to, and even a British band called 'The Human League' had written a song about the country. I can remember as a child, seeing in the news that a British journalist called John McCarthy had been kidnapped and held hostage alongside an Irishman called Brian Keenan. They had been taken and held by a group called Islamic Jihad, a Shia militia group, who are reportedly responsible for many bombings and kidnappings in Beirut in the 1980's. In 1987, a year after John McCarthy's kidnapping, the Arch Bishop of Canterbury had sent a 'Peace Envoy' called Terry Waite out to negotiate the release of the hostages and he ended up getting kidnapped and held himself. Keenan was released in 1990 and McCarthy and Waite in 1991 respectively. All in all, Lebanon and Beirut were etched into my mind as one of the worlds most dangerous places, which of course, it was for decades.

* * *

In the March of 2018, Penny Appeal had organised a trip to Lebanon with aid for Syrian refugees living there. The mission was to be lead by a senior producer, but due to him becoming sick at the last moment, the responsibility was handed to me. I was given the brief by my line manager, and headed to Heathrow Airport, where I met the rest of the team for the flight with Middle East Airlines to Beirut. The contingent consisted of myself, well-known fundraiser Faraz Yousufzai, and two other Penny Appeal fundraisers; Umran Amin from Glasgow and Khalil Benkhalil from Bradford.

The direct flight to Beirut took around four and three quarter hours, and we landed early evening. Going through immigration was straightforward for all us apart from Khalil. He is a British citizen with a British passport, but had been born in Libya and moved to the Uk when he was less than a year old. This suddenly proved to a massive problem. None of us realised that there is an issue between Lebanon and Libya, and no one from Libya is allowed to enter Lebanon and visa-versa, for reasons stretching back 30 years or more, and compounded by Lebanon's decision to enforce a no-fly zone over Libya in 2011 on behalf of the UN. The immigration officers asked Khalil a whole host of questions, even using google maps to ask him how many cars were parked on his drive and what colour they were. Four hours had passed with no joy, so I called the ground partner, who called the chief of police, who called the officers, who eventually let Khalil through. It had come very close to him being sent back to the UK on a flight but thankfully this had been averted.

After arriving at the hotel in Beirut and dumping our bags, we hit the streets to find a place to eat, then got our heads down ready for our first mission the next morning.

We were met in the reception of the hotel by our ground partner, Shaikh Ziyad of ACA (the Awareness and Consolation Association). Shaikh Ziyad was man of average height and build, and a shaved bald head like myself, and near enough in age. He had been a police officer for years, but had left that life to work in the humanitarian sector, and was doing great work for the Palestinian and Syrian refugees in Lebanon. We drove out of the city towards the port town of Saida, and around fifteen kilometres south of Beirut, we headed back inland a couple of miles to a small town called Ketermaya, where the ACA headquarters were. When we arrived, we were greeted by fifty children aged between five and sixteen years old, and a very large banner welcoming us. We connected with the kids and presented them with gifts, mostly sports games such as tennis racket, ball, footballs, cricket bats, and kites. A coach pulled up and the children, along with the volunteers from ACA boarded, and set off to the local shopping mall. This was the first time that I had seen such immense happiness and glee on the faces of the children. In fact, any children I had filmed since I started out in the charity sector in 2016. They were given free reign to pick a couple of items of clothing from the store we were in, and Faraz, Khalil and Umran helped the children choose, albeit with a lot of larking around and laugher.

The next part of the day out was to a restaurant called Jododona (our grandfathers) restaurant at Daraya Town beside the Hamam River. It nestled in a valley with steep forested hills on either side, and the river ran alongside the wall of the restaurant itself. It was late spring so the leaves were all fresh sprouted and bright green, with the sun highlighting them even more.

The food came and a magnificent array of plates of grilled meat and rice, pitta bread, hummus, babaganoush, french fries and salad. All to be washed down with litres of fizzy drinks. It was a treat for the children to have such a feast, and to get out of the town they lived in. Of course, the gratitude of being safe in another country, away from the perils and terror of war was always there, but this day seemed to be something very special for them. I noticed that the volunteers were exceptionally good. I have encountered many workers and volunteers in numerous charities around the world, and they have all been amazing with the children in their care, but these sisters took it to another level. The love and care toward the orphans were as if these were their own children, Alhamdulillah.

Our final stop was at Birak Park, a fairground up in the hills. By the time we arrived, it was already dark, and the lights of the rides were twinkling in the cold spring night air. The temperature had dropped considerably and everyone was getting cold. Except for the children of course. They rushed in like kids in a sweetshop. There were roundabouts, slides, a large ferris wheel and of course the bumper cars, or dodgems as they are commonly known. That was the most fun, and we all had a go, pairing up with some of the children. I got onto the Ferris wheel to film the children enjoying themselves and get some arty camera angles, not thinking about my fear of heights. The wheel turned and I eventually rose to the top. Then it stopped. And stayed stopped! It was really cold by this point, and there seemed to be an issue with the motor, or so I thought. The kids loved it, and it was as I was starting to get agitated, that the wheel rolled into motion once more. In my sometimes oblivious mind, I hadn't factored in that for someone to get on to the wheel, it would need to stop for every person. It just took a while.

Returning to the coach, we welcomed the warmth of the interior, and made our way back to the ACA headquarters. From there, we checked into a new hotel in the seaside town of Saida. Our hotel was an old converted castle, with huge stone blocks forming the walls with really high vaulted ceilings. It was one of the defending walls of the castle from the thirteenth century. A truly beautiful location.

Day two was focusing on the mothers of the orphans. It was a very well thought out programme, giving the ladies the opportunity to interact socially with one another and form meaningful bonds outside of their lives with their children. Most of them had lost their husbands in the war in Syria and were effectively alone with their children, with little or no support, other than that of ACA. The first activity was arts and crafts, where the mums made all sorts of items, from scarves, hats and clothing, to greetings cards, post cards and paintings. We were taken to the house of one of the mums who had a sewing machine supplied by the charity so that she could make items of clothing to sell to bring more money into the household. It didn't bring in a lot of money but it definitely helped. This was a complete contrast to the refugees I had encountered on my first ever humanitarian mission to Greece in 2016. At least here they were able to do something to help themselves.

We left once more by the same coach we had been on the day before, and headed up into the hills. Lebanon is a beautiful country, and we were there just after the trees had blossomed, so it was reasonably luscious in places. The hills are terraced and with many houses set into the landscape. At one roundabout, there was a monument of a man and woman stood on top of a huge boulder, holding their guns up in the air in a sign of defiance and victory. The country had seen so much war and strife over the years, yet there was a calm and peaceful atmosphere all around.

We arrived at our destination, which was a medieval castle in a place called Mont Liban. Sandstone yellow, it rose out of the hillside like a vast fortress, stark against the bright blue sky. All around it were steep gulleys, ravines and forest, coming up to the castle walls. The walls still had razor wire around them, especially on the parapets that the public could access. In one spot, I stood on the edge and could see down the boulder strewn slopes below, with razor wire separating from a possible fall to ones death. The view along the valley into the distance was breathtakingly beautiful, with hills climbing either side and a river meandering along the valley floor. Faraz stood up on the edge of the parapet and I took an epic photo of him. The mothers were all heading inside the castle for a tour of its rooms' corridors. We walked though a door and out into a huge courtyard with a fountain and pool in the middle. The mums talked and laughed and I could see how important it was for them to have this time away with other young mothers. The sparkle in many of their eyes was priceless, as not forgetting the terror they had lived through and escaped from in Syria, they were also widows having lost their husbands in the war.

Lunch was at the same restaurant from the day before, and the final act of the day was a cooking utensil and food pack distribution to these mums when we returned to Ketermaya.

The third day was going to be a big one, as we were going to head out to Arsal refugee camps in the north east of the country. We had to be up early as Shaikh Ziyad was picking us up and driving us there. In fact every morning we had to be down in reception at a certain agreed time. Generally it was 9am, and the first two mornings, Faraz, Khalil and Umran were down with me at the same time. Usually ten to fifteen minutes early. However on this morning, there was no sign of Faraz at nine am. Or nine fifteen am. So I called him and he was unwell. Quite unwell in fact and when he eventually came down the stairs, he was a grey green hue. We had a talk and I suggested that he stay at the hotel and we would go without him, but he flatly refused. He didn't want to let the refugees down and in his eyes, he had come all this way, he wasn't going to let a bout of sickness get in the way. We jumped in the vehicle and set off for Arsal.

On the drive there, I was genuinely concerned for Faraz. His colour was pale green grey still, and he had taken some medication and was waiting for it to kick in. He eventually fell asleep for the majority of the journey and when we arrived in Arsal a few hours later, he had perked up.

There were bullet holes in the glass of the doors and windows, which had apparently been caused by Syrian gangs and Lebanese police in the days before. Arsal is set upon a sprawling high plain of hills with white tents stretching in all directions as far as the eye can see. They are clumped into mini camps but amass to around 100,000 people or thereabouts. Once we had taken on water and some snacks, we headed to a small warehouse by the side of the main road. Here were hundreds of boxes with Penny Appeal stickers on them, basic food packs with tins of tomatoes, chickpeas, rice, pasta, oil, sugar, herbs and other staple food items. There was a small crowd of people gathered around the truck, and it wasn't clear who was actually supposed to be helping load and who was a curious spectator. Once loaded, the truck slowly drove up a long slight gradient towards the camps. As we drove through, we could see the conditions people were living in. Some tents had UNHCR logos on the side, others had none and seemed like cobbled together tent-half hut shelters. The ground was soft still and we were told that the winter had been really harsh and it was only now, with the warm and dry spells, that the ground was no longer like a quagmire. The red earth was spattered up the sides of the tents and shelters and the people we saw were wrapped up warm and reluctant to come outside. This was probably a good thing. We weren't stopping to help them, as our agreed and planned camp was half a mile away.

By the time we arrived, children started to come towards us. A young man pointed at the side of the truck and attempted to say 'Penny Appeal', but what came out was 'Pineapple!' to my absolute delight! Grinning from ear to ear, they followed us through the camp until the truck stopped, and Shaikh Ziyad had a list of people we were taking the boxes to. In this particular camp, there was a box provided for every household. Khalil and Umran were there on the back of the truck, handing down boxes to the waiting families. What surprised me the most, was Faraz. After looking like he was about to expire on the journey up to Arsal, he was now stood on the back of the truck with the guys, and energetically lugging the boxes off the back to the patiently waiting beneficiaries. Ever the professional and with an unwavering commitment to the cause, Faraz did us all proud, in spite of his poor health that day.

Once the boxes had been unloaded, I caught a glimpse of Umran out of the corner of my eye. He had wandered off alone between the tents away from everyone, and was very upset. This was his first experience of a refugee camp, and understandably it had affected him. He took a minute to gather his composure, and then rejoined us as Shaikh Ziyad lead us into a tent on the edge the camp. We ducked our heads to enter the tent, and before us stood an old lady and her husband was laid out on a makeshift bed on the floor. Other than Shaikh Ziyad, Khalil was the only Arabic speaker in our group. He spoke to the lady and their story was really tragic. Her husband was unwell when they left Syria, and when they arrived at the camp, his condition deteriorated, and he eventually had a stroke. He hadn't spoken for months and the only way they had survived was through the generosity of other people in the camp. The box we brought them was the first they had received in almost a year, and the reality of the situation suddenly hit home hard for Khalil. I was filming the conversation between Faraz and the old man's son, when Khalil removed his glasses and put his face in his hands. Now this was the guy who is larger than life, full of beans, energy and humour, so to see him start to cry wasn't something I was expecting. With tears streaming down his face, he stared straight down the lens and and shared how he was feeling. Sadness, anger, hopelessness and notably guilt. Guilt for not doing more. I resonated with this last statement, as many times I had felt the same thing in the field. I was touched by his humility and bravery in that moment. Brave to keep speaking to camera as I could see he needed to articulate how dire the situation in the camps were, and that what we do is a drop in the ocean. As this was happening, the old man sat up on his bed and uttered some words. I can't remember what he said, but it was something like Alhamdulillah or SubhanAllah. This in itself was a miracle. The son, who was in his forties, hugged Faraz and he was so grateful for the food box we had brought.

We spent another half an hour in the camp, speaking with the residents, playing football with the children, and after stopping at another small group of buildings to drop more food boxes off and do some presenter links with the guys, we made our way back to Beirut.

Back at the hotel, I went to everyone's room individually and interviewed them on how the day had gone and how they felt about it. Everyone said the same thing, that the need of the Syrian refugees in those camps is almost an acute emergency. That more needs to be done. Sadly this tends to be the case everywhere, however even if it seems like a drop in the ocean, the work that NGO's and charities undertake in Lebanon does make a small difference, and that is what makes it worth while.

Our final day was spent walking around the city of Beirut, and exploring the steep hills and winding roads that lead from the elevated city down to the vast open sea front that stretches from north to south. Beirut is a strange mix of cultures and history: The buildings range from ancient Roman to Ottoman and then twentieth centre sky scrapers. We walked from the hotel down through the streets, past the university, and along in front of the American Embassy. There was a visible police presence everywhere, as there had been some unrest in the preceding months. Throughout the city, there were many signs of the traumatic history of Lebanon, and tensions were still bubbling away under the surface. This trip was before the three years before the port explosion, which killed 218 people and decimated the city. Everything was still intact back then, and there was a buzz on the streets. We set off along the sea front, taking photos and climbing down onto the rocks for a Team Lebanon selfie. There were people fishing all along the rocks, and the sea was kicking up a warm salt haze in the air. Wanting to grab some food, we climbed back onto the promenade. The only visible restaurant we could see, and to be honest had actively sought out, was McDonalds. This was one of the treats of visiting a Muslim country; a halal Big Mac! We ordered, ate, and dragged ourselves back to the hotel. I took some street photos of various graffiti and murals, and of a fascinating statue by the sea front. I would have liked to have spent more time in Beirut, but it wasn't to be on this trip. I wondered what thirteen year old me would have thought of my older self being in Beirut? I think I would have been impressed for sure, but also highly anxious that something bad was going to happen to me. Thankfully nothing did.

We had experienced a fulfilling three days of programmes and witnessed humanity at its best Ahamdulillah. What did stick in my mind was how the old lady and her husband in the camp had received nothing for a year. Abandoned almost. Khalil saying we all really could do more than we are doing. This comment was another seed planted in the future humanitarian forest in my mind; to think of ways and means to help more. A long term plan to start a charity specifically focusing on refugees.

10

Yemen

'Yemen is the largest humanitarian crisis in the world, with around 21 million people in need of humanitarian assistance, including more than 11 million children. Since the conflict escalated in March 2015, the country has <u>become a living hell for the country's children</u>. Only half of health facilities are functioning, and many that remain operational lack basic equipment. Many health workers have not received a regular salary in several years. <u>At least 10,000 children have been killed or maimed since the beginning of the conflict</u>, and thousands more have been recruited into the fighting. An estimated 1.7 million children are internally displaced. The damage and closure of schools and hospitals has also disrupted access to education and health services. More than two million children are out of school, leaving them even more vulnerable.

Meanwhile, Yemen has been plagued by one of the world's worst food crises, with nearly 2.3 million children under the age of five projected to suffer from acute malnutrition in 2021. Of these, 400,000 are expected to suffer from severe acute malnutrition and could die if they do not receive urgent treatment. In addition, around 8.5 million children do not have access to safe water, sanitation, or hygiene.'

Source - UNICEF

The visas for Yemen had been applied for in July 2017, and Riz and I had already paid two visits to the Embassy in London. After months of waiting, our applications had mysteriously disappeared, and we had to start all over again. Thankfully, our ground partner helped push things along, but it wasn't until nine months later in April 2018 that they were granted. My line manager, Martin Ball was probably fifteen years younger than me, but was also very efficient and proficient producer, manager and talented film maker and photographer. His humbleness, honesty and directness was very refreshing indeed, especially in a sector where people weren't always transparent or honest about their motives. He made sure I had all the kit I would need for the trip, and said if I needed anything at all, to ask him.

It was in the studio in Wakefield that I ran into another brother, Jawad. We were talking about the upcoming trip to Yemen, and he said something that stuck in my mind. 'You should have no fear when you go to Yemen, as one of three things will happen if you find yourself in the middle of some action, or being shot at. Either you will hear it, and not feel it, which means you are fine. Or you will feel it, then hear it, which means you are still alive to hear it which means you have a chance. Or you will feel it and then hear nothing, which means you are dead and on your way to Jannah as a Martyr in the line of work you do. So you really have nothing to worry about brother inshaAllah!'. Yeah nice one! Not that I was nervous enough already, but the truth in his words weren't lost on me.

Our flights were to Jordan via Vienna, with Austrian Airlines. On the leg from Vienna to Amman, I was sat next to a guy and we started talking. He asked me if I had been to Jordan before, and where I came from. I told him I was from the UK, a place called Bristol. His face lit up and he said his best friend had just bought a football club there. My face lit up and I replied 'Wael Al-Qadi?'. Turns out it was indeed and I had met Wael a couple of years before when I was making a promotional film for the club he had bought, my team; Bristol Rovers. The guy on the flight owned a food canning factory and was one of the main suppliers to the World Food Program and UNHCR, for refugee camps in the region. He gave me his business card and said to hit him up if ever I am in Amman again. Such a small world.

We landed in Amman, and when we got out of the airport, Riz and I took a cab to the hotel, where we had an early night. Our flight to Yemen was in the early hours of the morning, so we ate an absolutely amazing halal burger meal from a place across the road from the hotel and flaked out.

Yemenia airlines were a fleet of three Boeing 737's leased from Pakistan International Airlines. They flew three times a week, from 3 destinations; Cairo, Djibouti and Amman. At this time, there were only flights from Amman and Djibouti, and Amman was the easiest to get to from the UK.

I had been waiting for this trip for nine months. Dates had come and gone and the visas hadn't materialised. Finally, at the start of April 2018, the visas were granted and arrangements were made for the trip. Each time I had worked myself up to going, then was let down at the last minute, so when all was confirmed the adrenaline started to build. This was to be a very different trip from anything I had experienced before, and was a sudden reality check too, as I was now going to do the thing I had been most scared of; to fly into and film in an active war zone. I remembered the words of my friend all those years ago in media college; how her father had taken his own life from the horrors he had witnessed. The realisation that I might be shot at or even killed. I was told that I would be supplied with a flak jacket, kevlar helmet and would be travelling in an escort of armed soldiers in an APC; Armoured Personnel Carrier. Was I scared? Yes. Was I excited? Hell yeah!

In the preceding December, I had been to Iraq with Faz, Riz and another brother called Abdullah. This had been a bit nerve wracking, especially crossing the border from Iraq back into Turkey on foot at night but had been a buzz. Then getting stopped and questioned in the street by the Turkish military police the following day, due to three brits being a kilometre from the convergence of the Iraqi, Turkish and Syrian borders. We were released within 30 mins, as they confirmed our identities as humanitarian workers. It had been exciting and adventurous, but this however, wasn't comparable to anything or anywhere I'd ever been before.

As the wheels of the 737 touched down, it crossed my mind whether I would ever get to leave this country again. Morbid maybe, but this wasn't any normal trip. The civil war in Yemen had cost tens of thousands of lives.

The history of the conflict stems from hundreds of years of outside interference, and includes colonisation of Aden from 1937-1967 by the British. The British Mercenary Organisation had gone to the assistance of North Yemen, which was a Royal nation, who were fighting the Iranian and Egyptian backed Republican rebels. After this civil war in North Yemen, and increasing unrest and attacks in South Yemen, the British finally left in 1967, and the two countries were united into one nation in 1990.

In 2014, the Iranian backed Houthi Rebels took over the capital city of Sanaa, and Civil war has raged ever since. The coalition government is based in Aden and has the backing of Saudi Arabia, Britain and the USA. The balance of power and weaponry is heavily in favour of the Saudi backed coalition, and continued airstrikes of civilian areas, and infrastructure has now set the scene for a Cholera epidemic and put 22 million people at risk of malnutrition and starvation. The history behind the conflict and political power struggle is far more complicated that this obviously, and like every humanitarian, I can't and won't take sides, although my feelings on this are pretty strong, and the whole situation breaks my heart.

*　　*　　*

We waited in an office with some immigration officers who took our passports away. When our ground partner Dr Jamal arrived, he brought the visas from Aden that he had collected in person, and we were free to leave. It was 38°C and a very dry heat and were driven from the airport to our hotel. Along the route, Dr Jamal pointed out various buildings to us. There were grand hotels with huge holes in the front, one of which had been hit by F-16 fighter plane missiles as it had been thought the hotel was infiltrated with Houthi rebels. There were piles of rubble from buildings being completely destroyed, burnt out cars, bullet holes in walls and buildings.. although not as bad as anything I had seen on the news in Syria, it was as one might expect a city war zone to look like.

The hotel outer wall was peppered with bullet holes, which didn't instil a great deal of confidence in the security there. I have since been told that this hotel no longer exists, as it was bombed sometime in the last couple of years since the trip. The people carrier pulled into the hotel's walled compound, parked up. Walking into the hotel reception, I saw the welcome familiar face of Irfan. He was sat down drinking coffee with a long haired guy called Harun. Harun was working for Muslim Charity and had been in Yemen a few days before us. A really easy going brother, we sat and smoked cigarettes, drank coffee and talked about who we knew from the sector and where we had been.

It was here that Irfan called for my attention, as he needed to explain something to me. He had dispensed with the Armoured Personnel Carrier, soldiers, flak jacket and the kevlar helmet. I was absolutely gobsmacked. 'WHAT? WHY?!" I almost shouted in disbelief. This is where the wisdom and experience of Irfan and his twenty five year experience of working with the UN and other charities in conflict zones became apparent.

'The coalition' as it was known, consisted of three players; The Saudi backed militia, the Emirates backed militia and the South Yemen Separatist rebels. How it worked, for example, an individual would go to see a unit 'leader', who would give him an AK47, a months worth of ammunition and $1000, and told to patrol and guard a certain block or set of streets. Then they were told to come back next month for more of the same. The only uniting factor was that they all hated the Houthi Rebels more than they hated each other. So if an APC with Saudi decals drove into a South Yemen Separatist area, it would undoubtedly draw fire, putting everyone at risk. Same with the Emirates militia. In fact these three factions were having firefights multiple times a day in and around Aden, making it one of the most dangerous places on earth, alongside Syria, South Sudan and Somalia. Any kind of military muscle would have made the risk to us and anyone in our group ridiculously high.

The first area of aid distribution was in a South Yemen Separatist stronghold, so we needed to be incognito. A flak jacket had been provided, but again, I was told it would make me stand out like a sore thumb. Not that it was hard to do, as I was the only European or Caucasian in Aden at that time, or so I was told. Sat in the back of the people carrier with blacked out windows, between two of the ground staff workers, dark glasses and a Yemeni scarf wrapped around my head, we made our way through the packed streets towards the Medical centre. There were pick-up trucks with anti aircraft guns mounted on the back, with militia hanging off all around the truck, each with an AK47 and a cricket ball of Khat in their mouths.

The scenery was striking. Huge spiking volcanic peaks rose into the deep blue sky, surrounding this part of Aden like a crown of thorns. Eagles swooped down from the mountainous outcrops and the heat was almost deafening, if that makes sense. We walked into the medical centre and were shown around each of the check-up rooms. There was a room for general check-ups and medical conditions, and there was also a ladies clinic for feminine health and gynaecology.

Many of the patients were children, who were in desperate need of medicines we had brought in with us. Although we saw no real signs of acute or extreme malnutrition in Aden, children and adults were generally very thin, and the wartime environment was definitely taking its toll, both physically and mentally. Everyone seemed exhausted, and the children looked like they had witnessed multiple lifetimes in their short years.

Once I had filmed everything I needed, we headed back through the heaving streets and suspicious eyes of the residents. At the hotel we ate dinner, and swapped stories as per usual. My nerves were a little frayed as the energy there was different to anything I had experienced before. I think that the continuous strong teas and coffees probably didn't help, so the first night was a rather unsettled affair.

The next morning, we met for breakfast and headed out into another South Yemen Separatist area. The distribution was happening in a disused sports centre. As we arrived, we saw a truck being unloaded. There were sacks of flour, rice, tins of vegetables, chick peas, olive oil, sugar, spices and other staple food supplies.

I filmed all of this unfold and the locals come in one-by-one and collect their pile of goods. One of the men stood on guard outside, must have been around 6'4" tall. He looked like he was older than me, tall, lean, had a bullet belt strung over one shoulder and a heavy machine gun over the other. I went to shake his hand and he held it out to me, with his thumb covering the palm of his hand. There was such a look of mistrust in his eyes, as obviously there was I, a bald headed Englishman in front of him. I told him my name was 'Muhammad Abdul Mateen' and his expression changed immediately, with his thumb opening and a proper hand shake ensuing. It made me wonder how much damage the British Empire had done to this country over the generations.

It was just after this, that the sound of gunfire started popping off in the street behind the sports centre. I can remember when we first landed, I had wanted to see some action. Now I could hear it less than 50 metres away, and my outlook changed rapidly. Pop! Pop! crack! crack! crack!. We were ushered up to a first story room in the middle of the sports centre and told to wait there until further notice. Laid out on pillows and cushions, we could see the walls riddled with bullet holes just around head height. These were from a previous occasion, but were also a reminder of exactly where we were and what was happening around us. When working at TVC in Soho with my mate Simon Ward, or at Evolutions with the legendary Duncan Wilson, I would sometimes take a break and chill and stretch out on the edit suite sofa. This felt the same, but with a little more 'jeopardy'. After a couple of hours, we returned downstairs, the fighting had stopped and the danger had passed. The cooking utensils were distributed and I had filmed everything I needed. As we got into the car, I asked one of the guys guarding us for a selfie. He had a machine gun, and what appeared to be a British Liberal Democrats T-shirt on. Great advert for the Lib. Dems., and it really made me chuckle.

Back at the hotel, we could hear more fighting outside and the news came through that the Houthi leader had been killed by a drone strike near the Saudi border. They were expecting a rocket attack at any time and now everything had become more serious.

To top that off, the airport which was under control of the Saudi backed militia, had been attacked by the South Yemen Separatists. The attack had been repelled, but the airport was now closed until further notice. The last time this happened, it had been closed for three weeks. There was a real sense of worry, as Harun was due to fly back to the UK the next day. Irfan already had an evacuation plan in place if things got out of hand here. He had a fishing boat on standby in the harbour, to come to the beach by the hotel if an evacuation was needed. We would then cross one of the most shark and pirate infested waters in the world to the relative safety of Djibouti. Foolproof! What could go wrong?!

This was all starting to get to me and I could feel panic rising within. Everything started building up in my head; the death of the Houthi leader and the expected incoming rockets, the rumours that Houthis had yet again infiltrated the city and were about to attack, F-16s could respond accordingly and blow up any suspected hotels or buildings, the airport had been attacked and closed, and then the ever present risk of kidnap and even execution by the very real Al Qaida or ISIS.

I had gone to bed but couldn't sleep. Fear was eating me up and I just didn't know what to do until finally, it came to me. The only way forward was to be in the 'now'. The *here and now*. I had to shut everything out that was outside the hotel. Home, kids, work, war, danger, life in general. All I needed to focus on was right 'here and now', and where I will be for the next hour. Anything before or after that just didn't exist. Drinking coffee and strong tea and chain smoking cigarettes, until it was time to look at the next hour. This was everything right now. And it was quite a buzz to free oneself from everything else and just be in the moment... and then I fell asleep.

Amazingly, the airport reopened the next day and Harun managed to fly out unhindered. In the afternoon, Riz, Irfan and I went to visit an old peoples home, that had formerly been a home run by Mother Theresa's charity. It had been attacked by Islamic State fighters only eleven months earlier and the inhabitants slaughtered. Many of the residents were suffering from diabetes and other debilitating illnesses. Some had been left when their families had fled the fighting, but often being immobile, they had been left at the home, with the hope that they would be looked after.

It was quite upsetting to see, but it was also plain to see that the nursing staff and doctors were doing everything they could with what they had, and that the residents were being cared for as best they could. We were shown around the garden, where vegetables were growing and animals kept. One of the residents picked a lime from the tree and gave it to me. We left shortly after and as we stepped into the car, another firefight started at the end of the street. Between whom, I had no idea, but all I knew was I didn't want to be right there at that moment in time. We left hurriedly in a different direction.

During the night I could hear a mosquito in my room, but couldn't see it. The high pitched whine, coming and going around the room, above my head, then next to my ear, always left me feeling anxious as they would always find a way to get to me. I woke the next morning with what I thought was a peppercorn on the pillow next to me. It was actually a fat over engorged mosquito who had feasted on my blood a little too much and had perished as I rolled in my sleep. The mirror revealed the full extent of its feast, as I faced myself with a bumpy face, nose, cheek and head. And it had started to itch like hell and of course, I scratched making matters worse. I googled what could make the swelling go down, and it turned out that fresh lime juice could reduce swelling and itching. As if by divine planning, I reached into the side pocket of my camera bag, and there it was, the green lime given to me the day before. It did the trick. I washed it off before going onto the sunlight again as apparently, this can cause the skin to blister if left on.

We drove in convoy out of the city, past army bases and rumbling columns of trucks and APC's decked out with heavy duty firepower, uniform and kit. These were the Emirates militia, looking more like something out of an American war movie. Skull masks, reflecting dust glasses, over-ear helmets, and desert camo. Knowing when to point a camera and when to put it away is something I have learned on the job, and like so many other things in this line of work, it is a very fine line indeed. As one of the APC's rumbled past us, making the car vibrate, it pulled back into the lane in front of us. I was filming the view out of the windscreen through the gap in the seats, and the soldier manning the gun turret on top of it saw me, and levelled the heavy duty mounted machine gun down at me. Just a warning, but it did the trick. I whipped my camera down and stopped filming. It did put me on edge even more than I already was, so I stuck to filming the beautiful striking mountain peaks I could see out of the side window.

The village compound where the water distribution was happening was in Emirates controlled area, in the desert about an hour outside Aden. We drove into a gated compound, where hundreds of women, dressed all in black, many with niqabs, queued up to be given five litre water canisters. They were allowed two each. It was here that Irfan being the good sport that he is, joined in with the kids playing hopscotch, and ended up tripping and flying right into Riz'z nether regions. It was one of the only moments of comedy on this trip!

It was the time once more, for a water tanker lorry to fill up a huge barrel reservoir with water. This was another moment for me to hang off the back and get a great shot of the side of the truck, ploughing through the desert and kicking up dust and sand. I got the shot I needed, and then climbed up onto the top to film the guy pouring the water via a hose, into the reservoir. It was whilst getting carried away with this shot, with the beautiful, rugged mountains in the background, that I had't noticed the women slowly heading off one-by-one, after filling their cans with water. Panicking I would miss the main shot, I jumped off the top of the water tanker and jarred my left knee as I landed. This became the precursor to a physical injury which plagued me the following year.

After the distribution, I went for a walk with Dr Jamal through a neighbouring walled piece of desert, where there were two dozen or more crosses of British soldiers who had been killed in 1962. The British had introduced many good things throughout the world, but everywhere I went in my line of work, the colonial footprint and shadow of the British Empire or military was evident in one way or another. We packed up and left as the interest from the Emirates militia was beginning to border on the unhealthy.

As it was our last day in the field, Dr Jamal took us and the volunteers for dinner in a restaurant in Crater, the area of Aden nestled within the old volcano. The sisters were all young engineering students, studying at the university or recently graduated. They had been with us throughout the trip and were instrumental to Dr Jamal's charity operations. We all ate, joked and shared stories of our families and dreams. It still makes me feel so sad to know that due to geography, the lives of Dr Jamal and these sisters are very different to ours. This is one thought and feeling I have had and continue to have on all my travels.

In the afternoon, we checked out and headed to the airport with Dr Jamal. Driving though the city, looking at buildings blown up by mortar, machine gun and tank fire, burnt-out cars and bullet holes in just about everything, I realised I had survived what could easily have been a more dangerous and terrifying trip. Sat in the back of the car, scarf wrapped around my head and sunglasses on, we drove up the approach road to the airport. Dr Jamal and Irfan were talking intently about some other possible projects, and Riz and I were relaxing in the back seat. We went through the first checkpoint and the soldier put a cross on Dr Jamal's arm in permanent marker. We drove another 30 metres to the next checkpoint and the same thing happened again. To our left was the pockmarked wall to the airport and to our right were burnt out cars and the wreckage of what I think was a burnt out tank.

As we pulled up to the third checkpoint, Dr Jamal slowed down and looked over at the two soldiers. Both were chewing khat and deep in conversation. They looked over at us, and turned and carried on talking. Dr Jamal took this as permission to drive on, so the car moved forward. As we drove on, I saw from the corner of my eye one of the soldiers jumping up and running into the road behind us, waving for us to stop. I turned to the guys and said they should stop, alas on deaf ears. I turned once more and saw the soldier undo the safety catch, cock his gun and point it at the back of the car. The other soldier stood up and pointed something at us which I can only presume was an RPG. In absolute terror, I screamed out 'STOP!'.

The car ground to a halt and time stood still for a few seconds… two, three, four, five, six, I counted inside my head. I was waiting for something to happen; either feel bullets ripping through us or the impact of rocket propelled grenade… In this moment, I remembered the words of brother Jawad.. 'If you feel it but don't hear it, you're going straight to Jannah!' The only way I can explain it is that it was a momentary acceptance that I was about to die. No drama, just a cold simple fact.

Death never came…. no bullets or grenade….and it was gone again in the next breath. Very matter of fact, but I was still alive alhamdulillah.

The car reversed up to the checkpoint we had just passed, and there was a lot of shouting between Dr Jamal and the soldier. Everything was in order and we proceeded into the airport car park itself. It was here I realised, that if I had been asleep at that point, we would definitely all be dead now. Not spending too much time on that thought, I took a selfie with Riz and Irfan, said goodbye to Dr Jamal and entered the airport building. Once through security, we sat eyeing the plane through the departure lounge window.

Embarking was quick and we were sat at the back of the aeroplane. My seats head rest had no cover, just bare metal, but I really didn't care about that, by this point. I was eager to get off the ground and into the air. As we took off, the flight circled the ring of volcanic mountains and the sprawl of houses that ran down the slopes. The sun was setting and looked beautiful as it hid behind the huge black and grey clouds on the horizon. Two hours later, we landed back in Amman, Jordan. The over zealous airport security tried to confiscate my brand new unopened pack of batteries I'd picked up on my way out from London. I gave the guy a look like 'what are you actually doing mate?!', and he decided against confiscating them.

It's all a blur from there back to the UK, but I know I landed at Heathrow the next morning and it was a miserable rainy day.

The trip had a huge impact on me and I wrote a poem about it a month later:

Aden

Creation of volcanic mountain
Gingerbread peaks ring around
Heavy metal blackened rumbles
Street to street a different sound

Stop and check, ok, wave on
Through dark glass to see unseen
Flip flop, canvas, Russian hardware
Salt pans, sea and kerosene

Tired markets, hours, days and years
The elderly bewildered eyes
Purity and innocence
Young stares have seen a thousand lives

This land, beautiful and complex
The knot and pull cannot explain
Didn't know how much it took
The place I will return again

Matt Robinson, May 2018

Even today, when I think about that moment, and how close we had come to death, it just sits there in my memory as something that just 'happened'. In fact it didn't really 'happen' at all, as we are all still here. Alhamdulillah.

Yemen definitely took a part of me and kept it there for another time for me to return. With the recent peace talks successful, and war now supposedly finished, I pray that the people of Yemen from all sides can get the help that they need, and a safer future without fighting. I had just had one of the hardest experiences of my life, in terms of fear for my own safety, but it was a real eye-opener into the dangers that people face every single day in a war zone. Just being on the street can be a hazard. Even going to get a pint of milk or loaf of bread can mean someone never returning home again. I count my blessings daily.

11

Team MC Tour of Bangladesh

'In Bangladesh, the number of street children has been increasing rapidly in recent years. Mostly, Dhaka city has been facing this problem due to internal migration and people searching for work. Hence, it is near impossible to count the number of street children.

According to the Bangladesh Institute of Development Studies (BIDS) projects, the number of street children stood at 1.5 million in 2015, and it will reach 1.56 million in 2024.'

Source - Dhaka Tribune, 18/06/2019

I left Penny Appeal in August 2018 to start my own film production company called Migration Films. I had also been invited to come on-board as a contractor with an organisation called Muslim Charity. Irfan was consulting for both charities and had put me forward to do the filming for them.

The first thing I did was spend three days filming with Harun, whom I'd met in Yemen. It was for a three-day London to Paris bike ride for Team MC, an events and activities part of Muslim Charity. This was a great introduction to a charity, whose work I firmly believe in, not only from a project point of view, but of the transparency of their operations, and of course the thorough due process applied to every aspect of their work. In the October, I flew to Bangladesh for the Team MC 'From UK with Love' Tour.

This was a full on trip and the itinerary was packed. After landing in Dhaka and the internal flight to Sylhet, we all met at the hotel and gave an introduction of ourselves on our first night. Fazlul Karim, Muslim Charity's Bangladesh co-ordinator gave a brief run down of what to expect, and how the next fourteen days would pan out. To assist me in filming was Anik, a videographer from Dhaka.

There were at least ten different projects we were going to be looking at, and also visiting some of the more notorious areas of Bangladesh. This was going be a very intensive two weeks, following each person and filming them on a different mission every day. Moheen Uddin was head of the Northern Office for Muslim Charity and was leading this trip. There was also Abdul Hanan, widely known as Coach H who was representing the London HQ. Coach H and I were to share a room for the duration of the tour, which was something I hadn't done before in this line of work. He was fine company, and put up with my smoking in the room, which can't have been pleasant for him, and taught me how to recite Surah Kauther during this time, which I am forever grateful for.

The first trip was to see a school in Mulvi Bazaar, which had been all but destroyed during the monsoon season. It had been renovated by Muslim Charity and we were there to officially re-open it, and add the finishing touches to the classrooms. Ranu, a restauranteur from Manchester was being followed on this day, and we filmed him putting the last licks of black paint on the chalkboards in the classrooms. After a few sit down interviews with teachers and a couple of the pupils, we all took part in some outdoor games, which involved running to pick up stones, place them in the middle of a large square area, then to run to the other side and then back again. It was hilarious and very confusing. The kids were amazing and we all had a lot of fun. We planted some trees for each person on the trip, myself included, said our goodbyes and headed for the Sylhet Tea Gardens for lunch.

This was a beautiful location, and it was my first time visiting any kind of tea plantation on any of the trips I had been on. For as far as the eye could see, the tea bushes covered undulating hills, interspersed with trees. Every now and then, we would see a couple of women picking the leaves or tending to the bushes.

We stopped at an old building high on the plantation, where lunch had been laid out for us. Chicken, lamb, rice, daal, roti, fresh chilli, cucumber and red onion; accompanied by the usual bottles of Pepsi or 7UP. During lunch, a small girl probably no older than four came up to us, and said she was hungry. Nurun from Birmingham and Hatice from Germany took turns in feeding her. This was the first time that Hatice had seen anyone living in poverty and she started to cry. This became even harder for her, as she didn't want the small girl to see how upset she was, so she smiled, tears rolling down her cheeks and kept on feeding her. Afterwards I caught up with her and got a few words from her on camera. This had indeed been the first time that she had seen any such things and the sight of the hungry little girl was too much for her. It was interesting for me to see the reactions of her and everyone else on the trip, most of whom had never seen abject poverty before. It reminded me of my first impressions of how people were living in the refugee camps in Greece. Yet this was different in the sense that it was due to poverty on a national scale. Perhaps I had become desensitised? I think to a certain extent I had, especially after some of the situations I had been in before, yet seeing Hatice cry suddenly brought me back to the stark reality of the poor child's situation. One of millions of children living hand to mouth every single day, and not knowing where the next meal is coming from. That's what I call a reality check.

The sun was getting lower in the sky, and it gave the landscape a warm golden tint. It was like being in a movie, with stark red, gold and green colours, all seen through a hazy humid lens. The further into the plantation we went, the more it felt to me like we were in a period drama movie set. Ladies in Saris and Hijabs, tending to the tea bushes, faces and forearms almost black from daily exposure to the strong sun. The sound of crickets and thick hot air, that could almost be cut with a knife. Another moment of realisation; where I was and what I was doing, deep in the Sylheti countryside in the midst of a tea plantation. Alhamdulillah. We finished our tour of the plantation, and headed back to the hotel ready for the next day's activities.

The following day, we set out in some Tuk Tuk's for AK School for the Blind near the centre of Sylhet. For the duration of the day I was following Coach H, as the school for the blind was something very close to his heart. His mother had been blind for many years before she passed away, and we knew it was going to be an emotional visit.

We arrived and were shown into a room where there were blind boys and girls in their teens. They were playing instruments and singing and it was a beautiful moment. One of the boys had learned to recite Qur'an by listening to it through a novelty drinks can speaker. Through listening over and over again, he had perfected his recitation and learned the entire Qur'an, becoming known as a 'Hafiz'. This was too much for Coach H, and he suddenly stood up and left the room. I could see tears rolling down his face as he walked away from me down the corridor, so I followed him. This is always good content for any documentary, as human emotion makes good viewing and helps to tell a story. However, it is always a very fine line between conveying emotion and exploitation of an individual or situation. I decided to stop filming and give him the space and dignity he needed.

* * *

Our brief time in Sylhet was over and the group headed into Dhaka. It was here that we saw some of the vital work that Muslim Charity are doing on the ground in action. Muslim Charity were working with Apon Foundation, who help to rescue street children and either reunite them with their families or find a permanent home for them. We met in the Thikana Centre, a children's home in Gulshan 2 district, where the children's ages ranged from four to late teens, and many of them had either run away from domestic abuse, or relatives had died or they had made their way to the capital to find their fortune. Sadly this never turned out the way as they expected it, with drugs, exploitation and sexual abuse being rife. One boy that had been rescued by the team in the preceding days, had had an argument with his father, had run away to spite him and jumped on a train passing by his village. It was one day's ride into Dhaka and he was too small to remember the name of the village where he had come from. He did know the district, so the team had spent hours tracing the railway line back northwestward on a map, trying to find a name that he recognised. They had no luck, but they were still trying. There was also the hope that his father would report him missing to the local police, but that as yet hadn't happened.

We headed to Airport Railway Station in the centre of Dhaka, and it too was like walking onto yet another film set. There were people everywhere. Sat around the station, walking, sleeping, eating, praying. A train came into the station and it was just like something from the movies. People hanging off the sides, sat on the roof, leaning out of windows and stood between the carriages. They were walking across the tracks, sat on the tracks, playing on the tracks. Just people everywhere.

I was filming Nazmul and Farhad on this day, and as we made our way through the station, we saw many children sleeping on the benches, on the ground curled up, or wandering around aimlessly. One lad came up to us and started to interact, laughing, joking and singing. It immediately became apparent that he was high on something. Sadly, one of the ways that these street children would cope, was to buy a kind of shoe glue mixed with a solvent, and get high on the fumes. Not only would this give them a high to help forget their situation, but also to stave off hunger. The centres policy was to not rescue a child on drugs for a number of reasons, one of those being the safety of the other children in the centre. All they could do was tell him to clean up and then they could help. Nazmul, a Paramedic from East London, was approached by another boy who was looking to be helped. He had run away from his mother, but was now regretting it, but had no way of getting back to her, or knowing how to get to her village. His name was Abdullah, and the first port of call was the Gulshan 2 police station, where he was registered and cross-checked to see if he had been reported missing. After this, we took him to the Thikana Centre where he was introduced to his new family of brothers and sisters.

In the afternoon, we went back to the railway station, where Farhad met another boy and amazingly, he too was looking to be rescued from the streets. He had been living rough for five months and had had enough. On the way home from the police station, Fazlul Karim received a call from the Thikana Centre, saying that the mother of Abdullah, the boy who had been rescued earlier in the day, had been found and was on her way the the centre now. It was such a miracle. To be rescued in the morning and his mother to be located by the evening was unheard of, so we rushed back in time for the very emotional reunion.

This wasn't always the case with the children rescued from the streets and many were never reunited with their families. The Thikana Centre was a temporary home until other arrangements could be made.

Over the course of the next ten days, I filmed the fundraisers visiting numerous projects; Ikhlas visiting a school in one of Dhakas slums; Sidulker at the Railway Slum, where people were living next to a railway track in shacks and absolute poverty; Hatice at Daulatia Daycare centre, which helped to look after children of the brothel's workers during the daytime; Dr Omar, at The School Under The Sky, which would take children off the street and offer them free educational classes during the daytime; Raj and Nurun cooking up a feast for the children at the Thikana Centre, and having a bit of fun whilst filming Nurun, giving Raj a bit of a Gordon Ramsey-style dressing down.

Through all of this, I was helped with the filming by Anik Bhai, as I would call him. Anik is a softly spoken true definition of a gentleman, with a great talent, not only for filming, but also for making anyone he comes into contact with, at ease. We have filmed on numerous trips together since this, and he is now my brother from another mother.

Having him there was a great support and made my life so much easier. There have been other trips, where other camera crews or operators have been present, and this more often than not, makes the job a whole lot harder. Cameramen walking into shot when I would film, or buzzing drones overhead, whilst I would be conducting an interview. Not with Anik.

It was a few days into the Dhaka part of the tour, where the toothache I'd been carrying for a month or so had finally got out-of-hand. I couldn't stand the pain anymore, so Anik took action and registered me at a dentist around the corner form the hotel. I really don't like going to the dentist at home, let alone anywhere else in the world, so I was beyond nervous when we arrived outside the building. Walking in, the reception was clean, 21st century and looked just like a newly built health centre in the UK. I was taken to meet Dr Lubna, who ushered me into a seat in a spotlessly clean, space aged treatment room. X-rays were taken and I was expecting the worst. I had root canal on half a tooth a year before, and the big hooked needle that had been shoved into the roof of my mouth back then, had almost sent me into orbit. I was dreading the same pain, but the pain never came. It was actually pretty painless compared to what I had endured in the past.

Two hours later, and after double root canal surgery, I returned to the hotel to rest and continue editing in the afternoon. This procedure in the UK would have cost in excess of £1600, but here in Dhaka it had only cost £160. And it was a far better experience, if there is such a thing where root canal is concerned!

The last project we were to visit was the 'Peace Home' on the outskirts of Dhaka. I was following Moheen for this one, and he had been for the grand opening the year before, so this was going to be an emotional return for him. There were upwards of thirty children in the Peace Home, which was the end-solution for those children rescued and taken into the Thikana Centre. If no parents or relatives could be found after ninety days, the children would then make a permanent move to the Peace Home, where they would receive an education, training and apprenticeships and be cared for in a loving environment, surrounded by their foster brothers and sisters and surrogate mothers and fathers who worked there. I must say that it was one of the most amazing and moving projects that I have ever witnessed.

Around forty percent of the children in the home were either physically or mentally disabled in one way or another. Often, parents couldn't cope with the demands and needs that came with a child with disability, and the children had been left on the street or had come to the centre another route.

The day was spent playing games in the centre, then a cricket match with the kids outside on some common land was one of the days highlights; England vs Bangladesh. In the evening, the children sang, danced, demonstrated karate moves and it was a in truly loving environment that we said our emotional goodbyes. Moheen was moved almost to tears just like the rest of us, and it had been a very special day to return to this life-saving home.

At the hotel, I conducted individual interviews on everyones' experiences whilst on the tour, and made a documentary film upon my return to the UK. It really had started out as 'From The UK With Love' tour, but the love we had all received from everyone we had met in Bangladesh, will be a precious life long memory for each of us.

12

Palestine Half Marathon

'In the State of Palestine, very few children of primary school age are excluded from education, but by age 15, nearly 25 per cent of boys and 7 per cent of girls have dropped out, and nearly five per cent of 10-15 year-old children and one out of three 6-9 year-olds with disabilities are out of school. Children from vulnerable households, children with disabilities, and 14-15-year- old boys are all affected by this system-wide barrier related to the inclusiveness, quality and equity of education services in Palestine.'

Source - UNICEF

In March 2019, I was to take part in one of the greatest physical challenges of my life; The Palestine Half Marathon.

At school, I was in the rugby team, swimming team, hockey team and running team, but my life had deviated away from structured sport over a quarter of a century before. My sporting life however, did have a renaissance. Ever since my teens, I had recurring dreams of scoring the winning try for Bath Rugby Club. A wild fantasy of course, and in 2011, after a chance meeting with a colleague in Homerton, East London, I took up playing rugby for Hackney RFC after a twenty three year hiatus. I had stopped playing in my teens due to knee problems.

At the grand age of thirty seven, I was playing blind-side flanker for the 3rd team. It was during my fifth game of the season against a hard team from Southgate Rugby Club, that I was spear tackled and sustained some serious head injuries, compounded concussion and ended up in the Homerton hospital. To top this off, I was banned from playing for twelve months, due to the concussions, and had lost my sense of smell as a result of this injury, thus ending my brief sporting comeback.

An MRI scan on my brain pointed to the fact that my Olfactory nerve had been severed due to the impact of the tackle, and I would be lucky to get three to five percent of my sense of smell back, if that. This has been the case for the last twelve years now, although it has also served me well whilst filming in some environments in the field, such as open sewers in refugee camps and rubbish tips in Gambia.

Doing this work all over the world had kept me in shape pretty much, as there is a lot of movement and activity involved. I had always been reasonably sporty in my youth, plus the fact I had been training and playing rugby in my late thirties. So when the opportunity arose to take part in a half Marathon, I jumped at the chance. How hard could this actually be?!

The first job of the year for Muslim Charity, was to film their runners and fundraisers running the Marrakech Marathon. I wasn't taking part in the run, just filming the event. There was a small contingent from Muslim Charity and a few of the runners became my adoptive sisters, the Khatuns. On this trip was Nazia Khatun, (Fitness Reborn UK), and her younger sisters, Sakira and Salma and we all hit it off and had the funniest time together. I adopted them and they adopted me, and we are now a surrogate family!

It had never occurred to me to do something so insane as run a half marathon, however the buzz and atmosphere of the race really got to me, and I endeavoured to sign up for the Palestine Half Marathon, with five weeks to prepare for it.

* * *

As I was fundraising for this event, I decided to make some videos of my training for social media. Being a fan of the Simon Pegg movie 'Run Fat Boy Run', I thought it would be amusing to have a play on words, and called the series of videos, 'Run Matt Boy Run'. My stamina levels were low and since my divorce in 2018, I had been living off an unhealthy diet of pizza and burgers, so I knew I had to do something about it.

The first was boxing training with Coach H in Muslim Charity HQ. This almost killed me and I couldn't get out of bed the next day. This was followed by; Gait analysis and buying trainers with Rashid Ali; looking at Marathon Mindset with Nazia Khatun; a 10K run with old buddy Charlie Dark and Run Dem Crew; finding out about the beneficiaries we were fundraising for with Harun; and the final film was an amalgamation of all the films purely for fund-raising purposes.

I was interviewed by Rukiyah Khatun on a show called 'Living The Life' on Islam Channel about the upcoming run. Rukiyah was another Khatun sister, and was also going to be taking part in the Marathon. Nazia, Sakira, Rukiyah and Salma became my 'Sistas with Blistas', in reference to one of the most common gifts of running. We would sometimes meet up for training, go on long runs along the south bank, and regularly meet for 'training' lunches in the Ottoman Doner in Whitechapel. It was like we had all known each other for years, had the most ridiculous sense of humours, and larked around. I don't think I had laughed as much in all my life.

The fundraising aspect was quite successful for my first attempt. I had raised £1700 on-line via social media, and a further £3000 from the generous congregations of Al Manaar Mosque in Westbourne Park, and West London Islamic Cultural Centre in Parsons Green; basically my old stomping ground from my days at Muntada Aid. I set foot on the flight having raised £4700 for the orphaned girls in the School in Shaikh Jarrah, East Jerusalem.

* * *

The flight landed at Tel Aviv airport and we proceeded to the Immigration desk. It was here that two charities converged; Muslim Charity and Penny Appeal. It was great to see some old familiar faces, especially Haroon Mota, who had previously run four marathons in four weeks in memory of his father. There were around one hundred of us queuing up to go through immigration and it wasn't moving very quickly. When it came to my turn, I stepped up to the glass-screened booth and handed my passport over. I was asked where I was staying, so I turned around and called out 'Rashid, where are we staying?'. The officers face changed, and he asked me if I was with the big group to which I replied 'yes'. He told me to go and wait over to one side. This happened to everyone and soon there were over 100 people waiting. Within half an hour, my name was called, and I was handed my passport and told I was free to go and pass through security. One other person got through, so we waited for the others. We watched group-after-group of people arriving from all over the world, coming through border control and into the arms of waiting families or tour guides. Everyone had Israeli flags, inflatable toys with the star of David on and other such merchandise. It was so bizarre and unnerving and the most nationalistic display of a people that I had witnessed anywhere else in the world. Seven hours later, the rest of our group came through, the reason for the delay, not given. Men, women, children, grandmothers and babies were all kept in that holding area, sitting on the floor for seven hours without reason. No food or water supplied. A shockingly inhumane and vindictive approach by the immigration force, and a fine introduction to the realities of Israeli hospitality.

Our coach pulled into the hotel in the East of Jerusalem, and I was absolutely exhausted. Everyone was going to Al-Aqsa mosque to pray the morning prayer, Fajr, but I decided to sleep. It was to this that one of our group, Rob Siddiqi, said 'you can sleep when you're dead'. This resonated and I joined everyone on the walk to the third holiest site in Islam, and one of the holiest sites in the world.

At the gate, the Israeli police told me that I couldn't go though, so I told them I was Muslim and that I was a convert. After a few seconds of to-ing and fro-ing, they let me through, just in time.

Al Aqsa compound is a large stone-paved area, with Al Aqsa Mosque one side of it and 'The Dome Of The Rock' the other. It was still dark, but there was a slither of light on the horizon to the east. We walked in through the giant main doors of the mosque, which must be at least twenty metres high, and found a spot on the red carpet to pray.

After the prayer had finished and the mosque emptied a little, a few of us went to the front of the mosque to where the Imam leads the prayer from. The spot was empty, so I walked forward and started to do a sunnah prayer. It was at this moment, that I realised the enormity of where I was praying; every prophet had prayed there, including the Prophet Mohammed (PBUH). I felt connected. The hairs went up on the back of my neck and I felt myself well up. It was truly emotional, and I had another one of my moments; here I was in Jerusalem, about to run a half marathon for Palestinian orphaned girls, and I had just prayed at one of the holiest spots on the planet. Alhamdulillah..

After a few hours catch up sleep, we all went to visit the Orphaned Girls school a short walk away on the edge of the Sheikh Jarrah neighbourhood, and were given a tour and a 'thank you' presentation by the pupils. The girls were aged between five and sixteen, and all smartly dressed in a uniform of grey trousers and red jumpers. There was a presentation of presents to the children, and then all of the runners mixed with them, asking questions about what they wanted to do in future. Some said doctors, other lawyers, teachers and entrepreneurs. All of these girls had lost one parent or both, so it was an amazing feeling to speak to them first-hand and to see that they all had dreams, in spite of what had happened to their parents, and the daily problems they and their families faced living in occupied Jerusalem. It was humbling to see what I had actually been fundraising for, first hand. I had always been a part of the crew, a part of the organisation, so to be an actual part of the event, and to see where all my efforts were going, was pretty special.

In the days preceding the Marathon, we visited a few places, including the Ibrahimi Mosque in Hebron. This was like entering Fort Knox, with barriers, fences and checkpoints to walk through. In 1994, a far-right American-Israeli settler had gone into the mosque with a semi-automatic weapon, and massacred 29 worshipers and injured 129 others. He was overpowered, disarmed and beaten to death. The atmosphere could be cut with a knife and it was very jumpy and uncomfortable. There was a man selling purses and gifts, who lived just down the road from the Mosque. He told me that the Israeli soldiers would shut the checkpoint for no reason at all, other than to cause difficulty and misery for the Palestinians. He would have to walk an hour around the town to be able to get to his home when they did this. Some streets they weren't allowed to walk down and front doors of Palestinian homes had been welded shut. Only Israeli settlers were permitted there, which was a clear example of the Apartheid laws employed by the Israeli government in the occupied West Bank. It was a stark reality of the illegal occupation of Palestine since 1967 by Israel, which western governments choose to ignore. These double standards, especially by the UK government and media, has been highlighted recently by the illegal invasion and occupation of Ukraine by Russia. Apparently it's wrong for Russia to invade and occupy Ukraine, but not Israel to invade and occupy the West Bank, and blockade and bomb Gaza? I ask myself how can this hypocrisy be so brazenly adopted for one nation and not another? Perhaps the BBC narrative is driven by the UK governments foreign policy, of having the heavily armed ally Israel, stationed in the middle east to regulate and keep relations between Arab nations weakened? Keeping them reliant on the petrodollar? This is something that the world is waking up to, and InshaAllah will be honestly reported on by the mainstream in the near future, rather than just independent news outlets and press.

After prayers in the Ibrahimi Mosque, we walked down into the market in Hebron, where the open-air alleyways had been covered with a canopy of chainlink wire fence. This is to stop the Israeli settlers injuring the Palestinians when they throw stone, rocks, rubbish and other objects at the market below. There were a few stones and a length of metal pipe suspended in mid air on the mesh. If they had hit someone, it would have caused serious injury or even death.

Upon our return to Jerusalem, and as we entered Al Aqsa once more for the night prayer, there was a commotion ahead of us. What seemed like a bit of fun from a distance, turned out to be a little more sinister the closer we got. Rashid, Muslim Charities Team MC Cycling Club Co-ordinator, had gone ahead to pray and was carrying a plastic bag with a Muslim Charity banner inside. The Israeli police had found this, taken it out of the bag and were mocking it, throwing it on the floor. The guy then took Rashid's passport too.

Seeing this, I remonstrated and was told, in no uncertain terms, to shut up or my passport would be taken, and I would be arrested. The absolute hatred in his eyes was chilling. Luckily, the senior officer was less of a tyrant, and gave Rashid back his passport and let us through into the Mosque compound, but held onto the banner and told us we could collect it on our way out.

This was one of many issues we had with the police at the compound. Many of them were from an Arab speaking ethno-religious group called Druze, who populate much of the middle east. Every time I walked in, I was stopped and told I wasn't allowed in, as my passport said Matthew James Robinson, and that wasn't a Muslim name. On one occasion, I had to recite al-Fatiha which is the Muslim equivalent of the Lord's Prayer, say the date I converted, where and who conducted the conversion. Another time, we had returned from Jericho and the Dead sea, where I had the honour of leading the evening prayer. I had my sisters sticking up for me and telling the police what for. It got so silly that I ended up ditching my baseball cap that accompanied me everywhere, and I donned an Islamic men's prayer cap. Amazingly, this worked a treat and I wasn't stopped after that. We did meet one policeman who came and spoke to us directly and was polite and friendly, which was refreshing considering the hostility we were meeting every day.

*   *   *

My room mate happened to be none other than Maroof Pirzada, head of Muslim Charity, his father Shaikh Pirzada being the founder. I had spent time with Maroof in the London HQ offices, but not spend any considerable time with him outside the working environment. Sharing a room was not going to be easy or fun. Or so I thought. I ended up having some of the best banter with anyone on any trip I'd been on; great company and a funny individual. We were also going to be competing against each other in the Half Marathon. I was determined to beat him, as even though we had a similar fitness levels, he was almost half my age. More importantly, after the winding up, we had given each other the preceding days, it was 'Race On!'.

On Marathon day, we all rose and prayed Fajr, then boarded the coach that would take us to Bethlehem. We drove past the huge wall that had been built and saw that there were two sets of roads; one for the Israelis and one for the Palestinians. Driving through the checkpoint, the coach stopped just as the sun was rising over the rooftops. We all disembarked and walked up a hill to Nativity Square. Rob Siddiqi was the only one of us running the full Marathon and had managed to get no sleep at all, due to people partying all night outside their hotel room. As we rounded the corner into the square, we were greeted with the sight of hundreds of people doing stretches and warming up, all to the sound of booming music from the stage next to the starting line.

The first to set off were the full marathon runners. This was great because it gave me the opportunity to film the start of the race facing the starting line, which obviously I wouldn't be able to get when I set off on the run myself.

Every trip I had been on so far, and every shoot I had done, everything had been filmed on my trusted Canon Eos 7D with Tamron Lens. This time however, I was filming on my Huawei Mate 20 Pro phone, fixed to a DJI Osmo 2 gimbal. It was the first time I had used a phone gimbal and it worked really well. The weight wasn't too much, and the battery life was pretty good too. I also had a go-pro strapped to my shoulder and my Samsung, for doing Facebook and instagram lives and stories. I was well prepared, and went around all our runners for some reaction soundbites, asking how they were feeling and whether they were ready. We all got together to take a selfie and for me to film everyone chanting 'Team MC' for the camera. My aim was to finish the race in one piece, or to at least cross the finish line and collect a medal, no matter how long it was going to take.

I actually felt very nervous, and was starting to think 'What the hell have I signed up for here?'. Before any shoot, even today after 25 years experience, I get anxious and nervous and my stomach starts to turn. So you can imagine how I was feeling at that moment; at the starting line of a 22 Kilometre run, with only five weeks training and preparation and having to run and film at the same time. The weather was still cool, and at 6:30 am the starting pistol fired and we were off.

It took around thirty seconds for us to cross the starting line, out of Nativity square, and a sharp left onto a downward slope. I could see all the names of our Team MC runners ahead of me; Nazia, Sakira, Rukiyah, Mehnaz, Josh, Tarek.. to our right was the sun, casting long sideways shadows on the tarmac from all the runners.

The course started to go up a gradual incline and whilst running and filming, I wasn't getting into a rhythm or pace. By the time I reached the huge 'Apartheid' wall, I was struggling, and it had only been a couple of kilometres. Again, I saw the friendly face of Haroon Mota, who must have set off behind us in the starting line up. I told him I was struggling, and he slowed to help pace me along with him. We spoke a little, but it was mostly words of encouragement and motivation. This was exactly what I needed at this time and undoubtedly, he set me into my rhythm.

We had been running along the concrete partition wall for a few minutes and this is where Haroon settled into his own pace and moved off ahead into the distance. The wall was a monstrous hulking concrete monolith, running through the top of Bethlehem itself. There was graffiti all along it, some by locals and others by rather more famous artists. On one corner at the very top, was a turret with blacked out windows. I wondered who was sat in there, and what they were thinking. From all I had witnessed so far, I had seen nothing but hatred from the Israeli military and police towards the Palestinian people.

In the years preceding my work in the humanitarian sector, I had been quite vocal around what I, and much of the world perceived as injustice and oppression, and I still refuse to stay silent on oppression and injustice today, as to me silence is complicity. However, in my job, I work as a humanitarian film maker, and that is the operative word; Humanitarian. I don't take sides. I remain neutral, impartial, objective as I can be in the situations I film, and independent of any political, governmental or religious bias. Most of the work I do is through Muslim faith-based charities, but I make sure that they serve ALL of humanity before I engage. If I see something I don't agree with that the charity is doing, I always speak up to whomever I am contracted to, although thankfully, this is a rarity. I try my best to stick to the four humanitarian principles; Humanity, Impartiality, Neutrality, and Independence. With all this in mind, the feeling of oppression and persecution by those in the tower and beyond, was suffocating and very real, and staying neutral in a situation like this in my experience is impossible.

I put that thought aside, as I passed a girl handing out bottles of water, opened the cap and gulped the contents down. This then gave me a stitch and I was struggling really badly. I trudged up another steep incline, past the Ayda refugee camp and I saw Haroon disappear around the corner in the distance. Wondering how Maroof was doing and whether he could keep up his pace having raced on ahead, I turned onto what I recognised as the main street, that I knew was a steady downhill for at least a couple of miles. Google maps had given me this information, as I had gone the whole length of the course online a week or so before.

People were lining the sides of the road, cheering, offering water and fruit, waving flags and children were running alongside us. I could see the full marathon runners coming back in the other direction. They had a shirt number in a red box, whereas the half marathon runners had yellow. The whole time I was running, I was filming, doing Insta stories and Facebook live broadcasts. As I ran past the 7km mark, I came alongside an old man who was plodding along in a steady pace. He was 76 years old and from Hebron. We spoke for a minute, and then I forged on ahead. I came across a couple who had travelled from Chicago USA, to run the Marathon. They said they felt they needed to come and run for Palestine, and that this event was vital to bring people from the outside world to Bethlehem and Palestine.

As the course turned right and up another steep incline, I felt my legs turn to jelly and my stomach summersaulting. This was so much harder than I had imagined, and I didn't think I would complete it, and would probably have to walk the rest of the way. I stopped and bent over with my hands on my knees, rasping for air. I could go no further.

A voice next to me said 'Come on, you can do it!'. Turning, I saw a young guy in his twenties. He handed me a bottle of water and I gave him a halal Haribo strawberry, which had been given to me by the Khatun sisters on the coach ride to the starting line. His name was Boulos Hanania, a christian Palestinian from Bethlehem. We started to jog at a slow pace to get my legs moving, and carried on to the top of the hill, which was the halfway mark, where the course swung around to the left and downhill once more. Stopping every now and then, sometimes for me, sometimes for him, sometimes to put gel on our legs to alleviate cramp, we stuck together and became running mates.

I passed one runner from the Jamia Al-Karam institute based in Retford, which is the Islamic institution founded by Shaikh Muhammad Pirzada, Maroof's father and also founder of Muslim Charity. He must have recognised me from my training videos, and shouted 'Run Matt Boy Run!', and high-fived me as he passed, which made me grin and gave me a little boost. On yet another very steep hill long stretch, I saw Maroof about 100 metres in front of me. He appeared to be struggling and Boulos and I were catching him up. I called out to him and he turned, saw me and suddenly picked up his pace, turning around the barriers at the top of the hill to follow the course back down. I captured him on camera as he ran back past me down the hill I was running up, shouting 'Run Matt Boy Run', with a grin on his face. He knew he had the better of me at this point, but I wasn't going to let it go.

Boulos and I stuck with each other, encouraging and pushing one another when either of us had to stop or walk for a short distance. A passing time-keeping car dropped a Palestinian flag, which I scooped up and held in my left hand. My right hand had been carrying the DJI Osmo gimbal and phone with which I had been filming for the entire run, but surprisingly it didn't feel too heavy by this point. We had reached the last couple of kilometres, and my knees were feeling like they had been repeatedly hit with a baseball bat. Nonetheless, we kept going.

The final stretch past the Bethlehem sign and up the hill back towards nativity square, was crowded with onlookers shouting and cheering us on. I handed Boulos the Palestine flag and as we took the final right turn and the last 30 metres towards the finish line, we clenched our hands together and raised them into the air. It was quite a powerful and symbolic moment for the both of us. He had found me struggling and stayed with me for the rest of the Marathon, and we had helped each other get through, and are still in touch with each other today through social media. After I collected my medal, I saw that Maroof had already finished ahead of me, but after checking our times, he had only beaten me by a minute or so. My final time was 2 hours 39 minutes, and I had been running with equipment and filming as well, so I felt that the victory was really mine!

My legs were like jelly and I had to sit down and get treated for acute knee pain and cramp by a paramedic. One of our runners took the phone off of me and asked me how I felt at that moment. I replied saying that I had accomplished something I never would have thought possible, then I choked up and felt the tears rising. I put my face in my hands and cried. Not out of sadness or pain, but from a place of having overcome some serious personal issues that I can't explain. Yet another moment.

Nazia, Sakira and Rukiyah had completed the run and we waited for Salma to finish her 10k run. By this time the sun was getting high in the sky and it was very hot indeed. I was grateful for the early 6:30 am start we had been given and sorry for all the 10k runners who had started in the heat of the morning sun. It was magic to see her cross the finish line, which I managed to film, then all of us got together, and feasted on shawarma kebabs!

Unlike a few of the group who had left as soon as they had finished the race, we missed praying Jummah at Al Aqsa. But it didn't matter. We had run our marathon for the orphaned girls of east Jerusalem and that in itself was reward enough.

The next day I could hardly move and hobbled around the tour of Jerusalem and the Al Aqsa compound. It was in the cave of Mary, that I spied a face I recognised. One of the heads of the

Ethiopian orthodox church that I had met two years previously, on the flight from Addis Ababa to Dire Dawa, was there in full robes. He remembered me and we took a photo. Quite a surreal and beautiful moment. It was a lovely day and we all got a thorough tour of the old part of the city. The Khatun sisters, Tarek and a few of us did some shopping and were guided to a cafe that sold Knafeh, a cheesy, sugary vermicelli desert famous in Palestine. We filled our boots and made our way back to the hotel, packed and boarded the coach to the airport.

*   *   *

I had heard so many stories about the security at Tel Aviv airport and none of them were good.

The experience on the way in wasn't good either, but I kept an open mind and prayed that we would all leave without incident.

The group had gone in ahead, as I was having a quick smoke before the flight. As I walked into the airport to join the back of the queue, two ladies in uniform came up to me and asked if I would like to jump the queue ahead of the group in front of me. I said I was part of the group, to which they looked somewhat perplexed. A few minutes later, they came over to me in the queue and asked me to follow them. I was summoned over to a plinth to be asked some questions. The first few questions were straightforward; 'What were you doing in Israel?' To which I replied 'running the Palestine Half Marathon'. They then proceeded to ask 'who I was with', 'why I was there', 'How long had I known the people I was running with', 'did I work for them' and 'why I had chosen to run the Palestine Half Marathon?'. I answered these honestly and openly.

'It's the first Marathon available to me since I decided I wanted to run a half marathon'. I thought that this would shut them down finally. But no.

'Why would you only run for Palestinians?'.

'I would't only run for Palestinians' I answered.

'Would you run for Israel?'

'yes' I replied.

Then came the big political question…

'What do you think of Gaza?'.

I laughed and told her that was such a loaded question. Upon reflection, I wish I had been quicker thinking and answered 'He was a genius footballer, but alcohol ruined his life'. Instead, I replied the only thing I could.. 'I am a humanitarian, I don't take sides'.

The lady put a barcoded sticker on the back of my passport. It started with a five, which I subsequently found out means a person of immediate interest. I was told to wait in a particular queue for security, and was joined by every male on our trip, bar a couple of people. We were kept for over an hour, and I needed the loo. I asked one of the security personnel and was refused. Not one for giving up, I threatened to undo my trousers and pee on the floor if they didn't take me, to which they conceded, and I was escorted to the nearest toilets.

After this, we were taken to a cordoned off area, where my bag was taken apart and every piece of camera equipment swabbed and wiped. Full body pat down, X-rayed, shoes X-rayed and then after three hours, told we could go. The man who had been swabbing my camera kit was actually friendly and apologised for keeping me all this time. I said 'thank you' for cleaning my kit as I hadn't done a thorough one in 6 months!

We all managed to catch the flight home, and had completed something many people only dream of doing in a lifetime; Praying in Al Aqsa, The Dome Of The Rock and running a half marathon in Palestine. Experiences were shared and friendships made for life. It was truly humbling. I had also earned the nickname 'Biscuit Knee' from my sistas with blistas, but that is another story.

The impact of seeing first hand the oppression, bullying and brutality inflicted on the Palestinian Muslims and Christians in Jerusalem and Hebron by the Israeli occupation forces, led me to write another poem:

No Sides

Crested arms armed
Finger breadth twitch
Scrutinised human traffic
Pass up and down
Caps and scarves
Champion and subjugate

Ice, ire and ego
Manufacturing misery
Taunting ruthlessly
Humiliating overtly
These ones
Godless hoes

Treating humanity
Vermin fare better
Feed themselves
Sick with hate
Sick the irony
Of dangerous foreshadow

Banners billowing
Grotesque ghosts
Washed out
Hidden crimson
Sucked from veins
Spilling children's brains

Matt Robinson April 2019

Palestine has a place in my heart like no other country. It is the country that brought me to Islam, indirectly through the biased and unbalanced reporting of the British press through the years. I see the oppression of the occupation and the killing and subjugation of the Palestinian people by the Zionist state of Israel on a daily basis, and it breaks my heart. I am a humanitarian, but I will never stay silent in the face of heinous oppression. As the chant goes; 'In our thousands, in our millions, we are all Palestinians!'. After a recent DNA heritage test, other than English, Scottish, Irish and Welsh, I am also Eastern European, Viking, and to me, surprisingly but most importantly, 0.8% Middle Eastern, which I choose to believe is Palestinian!

InshaAllah one day, I will return to run through a free Palestine.

13

Pakistan Rickshaw Challenge

'At Muslim Charity we endeavour to lift people out of poverty for good, so the idea behind the rickshaw project is to give a needy family a means of earning so that children can go to school and they can have a better life with more opportunities. In the past year (2020-2021) we have handed over 12 three-wheeler vehicles in Pakistan and Bangladesh for different enterprises including pick and drop services, food trucks or modified to use as vans for fruit-sellers.

Funds raised will also support the education initiatives under our Children of the World campaign whereby we renovate primary schools in the developing world and equip them with improved infrastructure to better cater for the students.'

Source - Muslim Charity

The last trip I had been on was to Bangladesh with 'Read Foundation' in April 2019. After that, it was Ramadan, and then I developed a knee problem. It started out as just stiffness, then started to swell up and made walking very difficult. By August, I was unable to drive, was housebound and could only shuffle a short distance on a pair of crutches. I went for an MRI scan and it showed that I had Osteoarthritis on the bone joint of my left knee. This had been caused by running the half marathon in Palestine without enough preparation, which had compounded the old injury I inflicted on myself, when I had jumped off the back of the water tanker in Yemen in 2018.

I spent two months laid on my bed with my knee elevated, binge watching box sets, reverting back to my favourite pizza and burgers and sleeping. This was starting to have a terrible affect on me, not just physically but mentally. But just at the right time, Michael Maisey, a good friend whom I had filmed his book tour in July with, invited me on a 'Native American Warrior Weekend' on his land in Devon at the start of October. This was exactly what I needed; inner child work, sweat lodge, Wim Hof breathing and ice baths. I left there refreshed and full of hope for the first time in months.

A couple of weeks later, my knee had improved greatly. I had the honour and pleasure of taking my autistic son on holiday to Cornwall and Devon, taking in the beaches, forests, hills and local organic produce. Muslim Charity had decided that they would engage me on an 'as and when' basis going forward, so it was whilst I was away in Cornwall, that Maroof called me and asked if I would be interested in fundraising for, and taking part in the Rickshaw Challenge in Pakistan at the end of November. I jumped at the chance as it was also one of the most amazing projects I had heard of thus far in all the charity work I had done. Sustainability is absolutely vital in the charity sector, and so many appeals are for emergencies, food distributions, education and medicines to name but a few. This was excitingly different from the rest.

The plan was for teams of three or four people to ride the rickshaws through the Pakistan countryside, stopping off in various places to take in the culture and live the experience on the road. When reaching the final destination, the Rickshaws would be handed over to some carefully selected families, who would be trained in the upkeep of the vehicles and how to run them as a business, thus giving them a self-perpetuating ongoing income for the foreseeable future. Their children would be able to attend school and it would actually bring the whole area up eventually, through business and education. A very clever idea indeed and I was so excited to be involved. This was going to be a real adventure.

*   *   *

I had been fundraising at the local mosque in Edmonton to a generous amount of £1200, and running around sorting final kit checks and arrangements ready for the trip. In the spring, I had purchased a new camera for my travels. The faithful Canon 7D was in bad shape, and it was time to move to a make that was good for filming in low light, which unfortunately the Canon wasn't. Along with the rest of the filmmaking world, I had been waiting for the Sony A7Siii to be released, so I decided to buy a smaller cheaper camera until it was released. I settled on a Sony a6500, which had the capability to film 4K, and with HD up to 120 frames per second.. an exciting prospect. The best thing however, was the ability to film in low light without too much noise on the video. Feeling geeked out, I stayed up most of the night getting everything ready and my bag fully packed.

With a grand total of two hours sleep, the cab arrived to take me to Heathrow Terminal 4. I was flying with Oman Air for the first time via Muscat, with an uncomfortably long stop over of 7 hours, which I wasn't looking forward to. The flight was nice and comfortable, and as I usually do, I gorged out on film after film, knowing I should try to sleep. We landed in Muscat at 7pm local time, and I walked to the Duty Free area to sit out seven hours until the connecting flight to Lahore in Pakistan. As soon as I sat down, an announcement come over the tannoy saying that the 2am flight to Lahore had been delayed by a further six hours and would be leaving at 8am the next morning. 'Thirteen hours!' I thought to myself, feeling majorly dismayed at the thought of sitting around in the same clothes in the Duty Free area. I walked to the Oman Air help desk and asked if they could at least supply free bottles of water. When the guy behind the desk found out I was on the delayed Lahore flight, he told me not to worry, and that I would be put up in the Oman Air hotel inside the airport for my inconvenience. 'GET IN!' I thought. I was so happy, and it was a really nice hotel, a couple of floors up from the Duty Free area. I was given a large double room with full facilitates and vouchers for dinner and breakfast. I dined on the gourmet buffet, showered and had a very restful early night.

After a very healthy breakfast, I boarded the flight and within five hours, we landed in Lahore. I had a mix of emotions as the plane was coming in to land. The last time I had flown to Pakistan, I was on my way to get married and was a non-muslim. This time, I was Muslim but I was divorced. My ex-wife's father had passed away only six weeks before, and I had been doing the fund-raising in his memory. It was a strange time, as the family of my ex had treated me like a son and brother, so coming back brought up difficult feelings. Then there it was again. The imposter syndrome made a sudden and unwelcome reappearance after being silent for some time. Who did I think I was, coming to Pakistan after my divorce? After all, my ex-wife brought me here in the first place, and I was now returning on my own. What right did I have to be there, filming such an adventure? I felt shame, sadness and guilt momentarily, then I took a deep breath, stared out of the window as the flight touched down. I prayed and asked for guidance from Allah, that my intentions were right, and that I would do a good job filming and taking part in this epic life changing trip. After my prayer, I felt much better.

I was picked up at the airport and brought to the hotel, where I was greeted by my brother from another mother, Irfan. It was great to see him after so many months of being laid out with my knee and was so nice to be back in the field after six months of being in the UK. We ate, smoked cigarettes and drank tea, and I was introduced to brother Ishaq, who was a mountaineer and adventurer. Ishaq was a tall and very humble gentleman, whose feats belied his mild nature. He had climbed K2, the world's second highest and most dangerous mountain. TWICE!: Once aged eighteen and a second time a few years ago.

One of the team members of 'The Three Rupees', a name I had coined to the amusement of the others, pulled out due to unforeseen circumstances. Faraz and I had been in Lebanon together a couple of years before and we had bonded during our work in Arsal Refugee camp in the North of the country. This meant that it was just a sister from Leeds called Fowzia and I, so we press-ganged Ishaq into joining us.

There were nine Rickshaws with different team members; The Bandit Brothers, Lal2Fan, WolfPak, Rickshaw Rani's and The Three Rupees to name a few of them. Once everyone had arrived in Lahore, we took an epic 400 kilometre coach journey over huge hydro bridges, through desert, sand dunes and wide open plains, to a place called Bhakkar,.

We checked into our hotel and spent the first rest of the day being shown how to drive the Rickshaws themselves, which wasn't as simple as one might think. The right foot pedal was the rear brake. The left pedal was the gears. The right throttle grip was the accelerator. The left handle grip was the clutch. Or was it the left foot and right grip. No.. anyway, it was very very confusing and difficult to operate.

Once we had all had a go and were able to drive, stop, turn, brake and reverse, (which involved pushing a handle backwards and putting the Rickshaw into first gear; not at all confusing!!), as the sun was setting we headed off to a restaurant around the corner from the hotel for dinner, and then turned in for the night.

*　*　*

There was a team from Islam channel with us making a documentary, so all my job entailed, was to film and edit a one-minute highlight package from each day. Sounds simple, yet it became an absolutely exhausting undertaking by the end of the rally.

The final stickers were put on the vehicles, we posed for a team photo and then off we drove, clouds of dust flying up into the air. I did a little bit of filming, then took the controls of our Three Rupees Rickshaw. It was a real buzz! We all pretty much stayed in line, with the odd overtaking every now and then. Past canals, sands dunes, herds of goats, sugarcane fields, palm trees. It was a real mix of landscapes. There was a lot of stopping and starting as everyone got used to driving the machines, especially on dusty, sandy-rutted and cratered roads. It really wasn't easy.

About a mile into me taking the controls, I broke the brake pedal by getting my size eleven foot stuck underneath it, and pulling it out of its connector when I'd pull my foot up to hit the pedal. It took the support mechanics a few minutes to put right, and we were on our way again.

The biggest thing I noticed about being on a Rickshaw was that it was so open to the elements. It was almost like one was part of the environment around them. Connected.

We were wearing face masks as the air was full of petrol fumes and thick with dust. I was enjoying the scenery, with a canal to my right and a high embankment to my left, when I made the same mistake again. This time, the Rickshaw in front had stopped suddenly too, and I had no brakes, about to fly right into the back of it. In an instant, I flung the handlebars left to dodge the back of the Rickshaw Rani's, but was now heading straight for a tree. In pretty much the same movement, I flung the handlebar back to the right and the Rickshaw shot through a gap between the two, missing everyone and everything and not getting a scratch. Ishaq congratulated me on my driving and taking evasive action, but I was shaken up, so handed the driving back to him. We had to wait some time as the mechanics tried to fix it, but it was no use. I had written it off in the space of a couple of hours.. I was gutted, and insisted that I would pay for any repairs or spare parts, but thankfully it was only needed to be taken into a workshop and have the pedal re-coupled. As the others had gone on ahead in a replacement Rickshaw, I jumped on the back of a motorbike to catch them up.

I spent most of the rest of the day filming out of our Rickshaw, and jumping in and out of the other team's vehicles. At one point, Maj Hoque, one of the Muslim Charity Fundraising team almost killed us by going off the road into a rut and narrowly missing other vehicles coming the other way.

We did finally make it in one piece to a small town, and drove in convoy to what looked like a small festival of sorts. The sun was still fiercely hot and beating down as the Rickshaws drove into a large open sandy space, where we were greeted by a small band of musicians playing tablas, sitars and other instruments. Garlands of flowers were put over our shoulders and next to us was a truly incredible sight that I will never forget. A host of men wearing turbans, carrying large lances and all on horseback. It was like something from the 1800's or even pre-industrial times. They were walking round in circles, and then cantering up to the end of a very large sandy field. This field was surrounded by onlookers and at the halfway point was a small stage with chairs and a PA system. The man with the mic would make an announcement, and one of the lancers would set off from 200 metres away. As the horse was galloping at full speed, the lance would come down and with incredible precision, would spear a peg sticking out of the ground. It was absolutely breathtaking. I had never seen anything like this before, and as I was lying on the ground filming, I could feel the thud of the horses hooves as they thundered by. In fact I was told that I was probably one of only a handful of white man who had been present at this tribal gathering for the last thousand or so years. The girls were the first ever women present apparently, and we all ended up presenting trophies and getting photos taken. One of the lancers asked me to jump onto his horse and pose with the hat and lance. Of course I had to oblige, and had a rather gormless picture of me taken. A memory for life though!

We pulled up to the hotel in Layyah and settled down for dinner in a tent which had been set up for us. Unfortunately, the hotel wasn't big enough for all of us and we had to drive a hundred or so metres to another one. Even this was oversubscribed, so I ended up sharing a room with one of the group; a guy called Umair. What was funny, was that there was one double bed, and we would have to share it.

Umair and I hit it off straight away. A keen cyclist, he had been on the Tour De Pakistan with Muslim Charity earlier in the year and had been one of the more adventurous Rickshaw drivers on the first day, overtaking constantly and weaving in and out of the traffic. He had lived in London for a few years where he had been studying IT and had returned to Pakistan to live the previous year. He had a big black beard and a wicked sense of humour. Having brought me a cup of pink Kashmiri chai, he settled down and helped me with the edit of the first day. It wasn't easy as I had a lot of footage to look through and I was exhausted from being on the road, exposed to the elements, the filming and also the stress of the driving. By 2 am we had finished the cut and both passed out.

Our call time was 7am, and by 8am we were all back in the Rickshaws, heading off to Multan. This morning was different in the sense that everyone had got used to driving, and leaving the town turned into what I can only describe as a scene from Whacky Races. Everyone was overtaking, undercutting on the inside, some clipping others' bumpers and generally just absolute mayhem. It got so ridiculous, that the lead Rickshaw pulled over and we were all given a talk on safety and to not overtake unless there was a clear stretch of road.

Unfortunately, the Rickshaw Rani's broke down and we had to wait for a little while on a sandy road, where Rashid was practicing a long jump to see if he could jump over a small irrigation canal that ran parallel to us. Rashid had cycled with coach H from London to Mecca back in 2016 and was always game for a challenge. He was head of the Team MC Cycling club which regularly undertook rides around the UK, and had done London to Paris which I had filmed back in 2018. Luckily Irfan caught up with us and told him it wasn't a great idea, as he could injure himself, and the hospitals in the area were rudimental.

We set off once more and I jumped in with the 'WolfPak'. Syful who was also another member of staff had brought some water pistols with him and was rapidly filling them up and squirting the other rickshaws as they passed. It was hilarious to see the surprised reactions of everyone as they were caught each time they overtook. My team mates Ishaq and Fouzia were squirted and we copped a tirade of something that would normally come out of the mouth of a sailor, but it was from Fowzia. We were in stitches.

After a couple of hours of sandy rutted roads, camels, cane fields and plenty of dust, we rode into a small town and pulled over in the centre, next to a tea stand and mosque. The area soon filled with villagers, and we ended up smoking shisha and drinking tea with them. Harun took out his drone and got some amazing footage of us all, then we all prayed in the mosque and were given thirty minutes to explore the various street food stalls. Umair and I found a man who was making fresh Gulab Jamun, a Pakistani sweet, made from balls of flour, deep fried and then soaked in sugar syrup. These were my favourite so we bought a box of a couple of dozen and shared them amongst the crew. This was the second time I broke my street food rule, but this time there were no dire consequences.

I jumped in with Umair and his team and we drove alongside a wide canal for the rest of the journey to Multan. At one point, Umair and the girls missed the turning to Multan, so we did a u-turn in the middle of oncoming trucks, buses and cars. It was a nifty manoeuvre and within twenty minutes we had entered Multan itself. This was where I captured one of my favourite images of the trip. It was a family of six; mother, father and four children, all sat on one motorcycle, riding alongside us, smiling and waving. In the words of Umair; 'a beautiful city with beautiful people Alhamdulillah'.

I ate dinner on my own in the hotel room as I had to edit the daily update once more. As with the previous night, I finished around 2 am and passed out.

We had only been on the road for two days but it felt like much longer. An 8am start and we were on the road again, heading to the Multan Pottery factory for a guided tour. After the tour we went to the factory shop, bought souvenirs and headed back onto the road. I was feeling like death due to the lack of sleep and curled up in the back of the support minibus for the next few hours.

We arrived in another small town and stopped for refreshments and to pray at the mosque. On my way back to the Rickshaw, I was walking with Irfan, when a man came up to us. He was from the local school and wanted us to come and see the building, so we followed him between a couple of houses that opened up to a large school yard with a hundred or so children playing. He announced our arrival, and all the children cheered and ran up to us. It was probably the best reception I have ever received anywhere, and we posed for photos, said our Salaams and went back to the vehicles for the next leg.

By this time, I was back with Ishaq and Fouzia and the driving the Rickshaw once more. It was making a terrible noise and had lost a lot of power. We crawled along at a slow pace and It was a few more hours until we pulled into a farm where one of the gentlemen we had met on the first day in Lahore was there to meet us. It was his farm and he was developing the land for arable farming to help sustain the local community. He also kept cows for milking and we were all given a guided tour. After an outdoors dinner, I was shown the problem with the Rickshaw. During the day, someone, and we don't know who (yes it was me), had sheared off part of a large hexagonal joint that the drive shaft ran into, and it was going to have to go into a workshop again. I felt responsible, so I promised to pay for the part and repairs, to which Major Zubair Shah agreed. The drive to the hotel in Bahalwapur was in darkness and on very busy roads. It was a little hairy flying along in the dark; buses, trucks, vans, cars and motorbikes all vying for space on a fast yet jam-packed main road. We arrived at the hotel and once more, I settled in to my own room this time and edited until the early hours.

It was the fourth and last morning of the Rickshaw Challenge, and we were all lined up outside the hotel ready to go. A National TV news channel had come to cover us setting off on our final day, and they interviewed a few of us, including myself. We all said a few words about how beautiful Pakistan was and how amazing the project was and how much hope it could give to the beneficiaries.

Not far from the hotel, we pulled into a cotton farm, where people were hand-dying and weaving the most exquisite shawls. Another opportunity for souvenirs, so I bought a hand woven organic cotton shawl, like one worn by the men of the region.

We rode along straight roads, under overhanging trees next to a river for a while, then stopped off in another small town, where Harun got us to all pose in a sugar cane field for the drone.

The rest of the drive was dusty and hot, and the closer we got to Derawer fort, the more desert like the scenery became. This was Cholistan. We passed camels, herds of goats, sand dunes, all under the heat of a scorching afternoon sun. As the fort came into view, it was like a terracotta sand castle in the distance. The closer we got, the more impressive it became until the scale of it was fully in view. It stretched for half a mile and the walls must have been thirty metres high in places. The fort was built in the 9th century and had seen a lot of action over the years. It was an awesome sight, and as we drove through a gateway and into an open space in front of the forts ramparts, we set eyes on the finish line. All the rickshaws curled around into a line, with each beneficiary stood next to their rickshaw.

Major Zubair Shah made an announcement and talked about the conditions for each of the beneficiaries; they would run a business with the Rickshaws, put their children into school, provide quarterly business reports and school reports to show their children's progress in education. It was an emotional moment for us all and I handed over the keys to the brother who was taking The Three Rupees. I filmed the rest of the keys being handed over and took some soundbites from the team members. What I really wanted to do was follow the beneficiaries home, film their environment and living spaces, interview their families and children, asking how this would change their lives and the impact an education will have on their children's future. But there wasn't time. The schedule was packed and the sun was already going down. After much celebration and dancing to the beat of a drum, we walked up into the fort to catch the sunset and pray Maghrib. A perfect end to an intense four days on the road.

The coach was waiting to take us back to the hotel in Bahalwapur, and stopped off in the Cholistan desert for a barbecue, traditional music and some dessert. By this time we were all shattered and couldn't wait to get back to the hotel to sleep. I did the final edit and around 3am went to bed.

*   *   *

The next day was spent sightseeing and visiting a museum in Bahalwapur. The museum was fascinating, with artefacts from all of the local history. Obviously there was plenty of items from the British occupation of India, and it was in reference to these when talking to one of the curators, that I got an unexpected piece of his mind. I had casually said how sorry I was for what the British had done, which gave him the green light to lay in to me good and proper. 'You can never begin to apologise for evils that the British have done to this country'. I don't remember the rest, but I was taken aback, and wanted the earth to swallow me up. I felt very guilty, very embarrassed and very white. I learned a lesson that day, which was be very careful of your words when discussing colonial history, especially when hailing from the colonising nation. Have some awareness man!

After some photos posing on a steam train, we explored the market and then boarded the coach for a long drive back to Lahore. On the way back, we stopped off at a restaurant where one of the brothers treated us to a spectacular dinner as it was his home town. All this time, throughout the entire tour, we had been accompanied by Pakistani Police Commandos, each wearing a jacket with 'No Fear' written across the back. I had wondered why they were wearing surfing gear until it was pointed out to me that this was actually their motto. The commander of this particular guard asked for a photo with me, for which I gladly posed. He then approached Irfan and asked him if he remembered him. After a minute or so, Irfan realised who it was. It was one of the officers from the police academy who he used to see when he would go to visit his father there as a teenager. Such a small world yet again, and the beautiful crossing of paths in the line of serving humanity.

Lahore was very polluted and hectic compared to the open spaces we had driven through in the preceding four days. After a bus top tour of the city, we walked around the palace in the centre of Lahore. It was a spectacular place with views across the city from all sides. After this we all went our separate ways to various shopping districts, markets and malls to pick up some last minute presents to take home. Umair took myself, Sabah, Nisu and Asma to a particular mall for gift shopping, where we found what we were looking for. Well almost. Umair took me later that evening to buy a new suitcase to take all my spoils home with me. It was highly entertaining to walk through the streets of this part of Lahore, dodging people, bikes, cars and motorcycles.

Our final dinner was at an open air restaurant next to the palace, where each of us spoke of our favourite parts of the journey and best memories. It had been a real adventure, and for the first time properly, I felt I had really been immersed in the environment of a country. Pakistan was truly beautiful on many levels, and even though I was shattered beyond words, it had been another monumental life experience. The next morning, we left for Blighty.

14

Odds, Ends and the
Road Ahead

'What we do in life, echoes in eternity'
Source - Maximus Decimus Meridius, (Gladiator).

There are quite a few trips I haven't written about in this book. Not because they weren't interesting or rewarding in their own right, but because I have included what are to me the most personal, interesting and varied experiences of my travels. In this chapter, I will touch on a few of the experiences briefly, but also take a look at the lessons I have learned from my time as a humanitarian film maker thus far. I will also look at upcoming projects and some final thoughts.

*　　*　　*

Gambia

My second trip in 2017 for Penny Appeal was to Senegal and Gambia, to visit their projects there. I was in a group of people including Shaikh Madani and the talented and popular singer, Harris J. Harris, known for his hit song 'Salaam Aleikum' and also in many quarters as the 'Muslim Bieber' due to his boyish good looks and voice, was on the trip as a high profile fundraiser. We had visited many projects, ranging from village water wells, to orphanages. His maturity, great attitude and work ethic belied his nineteen years, and he was a pleasure to work with. As the trip came to an end, we were visiting a crocodile sanctuary just outside the capital Banjul, and at the entrance to the enclosure, there was a huge plastic crocodile. It was really well-made and the attention to detail was extraordinary. Harris and I posed for photos and leaned over towards it to get better and more entertaining pictures, when suddenly it moved. Jumping out of our skins and shouting, we were given the fright of our lives and both leapt well away from it. It turns out that it wasn't plastic after all, and its full set of well 'sculpted' teeth had been ready to snap-up one of the UK's finest Muslim singers. These creatures are a hangover from prehistoric times and they look and sound scary, and needless to say we approached every crocodile thereon in with extreme caution.

I suppose one of my scariest experiences was in Gambia in 2018. I had finished filming for the day and wanted to go for a swim. Walking down onto the beach, I looked to my left and saw a long stretch of golden sand with palm trees and breaking waves. The other direction was the same. So very beautiful. The beach was deserted and the orangey, yellow flags were fluttering, indicating that it was safe to swim. Gambia is situated on the absolute west coast of Africa, with nothing between it and Central America, thus sometimes having very strong undertow, riptides and large breakers. I ran into the ocean, and could feel the pull of the sea under my feet as the waves receded. Not giving this too much thought, I dived into the water and started swimming. For the first few metres it was fine, then suddenly I felt a strong pull outwards and away from the shore. My whole body was being tugged backwards and I was struggling to fight it. I felt a primitive fear rise inside me and panic started to set in. I dived below the surface and it was even worse there, so I started to front crawl as hard and fast as I could. In probably less than thirty seconds, I was back into shallow waters and wading, legs and arms shaking back up the beach towards the hotel. The guy sat in the lifeguard chair asked my why I had gone into the sea on a red flag day. 'Red flag? What red flag?!' I retorted in disbelief. It turns out that the orangey yellow flags were actually red, but had faded in the sun. I did wonder why he didn't stop me or jump in to save me, but it was all so quick, I suppose he wouldn't have had time to react. Then I was out of the water, and everything was ok. I had a very lucky escape that day, and it could easily have ended another way, but it didn't, and the flag situation did make me chuckle. Now I check with the lifeguard of any beach I visit before I go in.

Iraq/Kurdistan

One of the strangest experiences during my travels, was the emergency response visit to Iraq after an earthquake in December 2017. It was a very long drive through the north of the country avoiding Mosul and Erbil, staying in a town called Sulaymaniyah, surveying the damage to the infrastructure, a semi-collapsed hospital, and giving out emergency aid packs to families.

Driving back again, the traffic queue to cross the border back into Turkey was a kilometre long and apparently 12-14 hour waiting time, so the ground partner had a car waiting on the Turkish side and we got out and started to walk. After an hour or so of navigating the border control, we started to cross the border on foot. It was around midnight and some guy that looked like Danny DeVito grabbed a couple of our bags, and started screaming and shouting at the border guards. Faz and I thought he must have been some kind of Don, but it turns out he was the manager of an Iraqi football team so they let him and us through. We crossed a bridge over a wide river and knew when we had reached Turkey because the paintwork changed from yellow and green to red. The following day we were detained by the Turkish Military Police for a short time until it was proven that were were there on a humanitarian work trip. Still, three guys from the UK with beards crossing over from Iraq on foot at night, next to the Syrian border, must have looked a bit dodgy. The strangest thing about it was upon returning to the UK. Every trip I had been on prior, whether to Munich or Myanmar, I had been questioned at a desk upon my return to the UK. The chip in my passport was broken so I would have to go to a desk, where I was asked where I had been, who with, the purpose of my visit, did I meet anyone there etc. Without fail. So after visiting Iraq and being security checked by the Turkish Military Police, I was expecting to get some special attention or even a visit to the UK's anti-terror HQ Paddington Green police station for questioning. After landing at Heathrow airport, I handed the border force guy my passport, he scanned it, and without a word, just waved me through. The same happened to Faz and Abdullah in Manchester. I have been told that this means that we must be on some kind of security list as humanitarian workers, but even today I'm still unsure.

Bangladesh

When I was with 'Read Foundation' in Bangladesh, on the way to the Rohingya camps, our air-conditioned minibus broke down. The driver tried and tried to get the engine started to no avail, so we jumped in a Tuk Tuk Rickshaw, and went the remaining eight kilometres open to the elements. It was actually a real eye-opener in the sense that there was no tinted glass between us and the environment. Like the Rickshaw Challenge, we were completely open to all the sights and sounds. I got an eye level view and feeling of the camps as we drove through them like I never had before.

After we had finished filming and returned to Cox's Bazaar, I ran into the sea fully clothed. It was magic. I did this on my last trip Bangladesh too.

The last trip was to Bangladesh in October 2020 with CAP Foundation, a UK based charity. All of the work we filmed was in and around the Northern City of Sylhet. Here were some amazing projects; such as a community corner shop, which gives income to a family and supplies the village with produce that they need on a daily basis; water well projects; Mosque building projects; and for me, one of the best was Fish4life, where a family is given a boat and all the fishing equipment so they can become self-sufficient. It reminded me of the same ethos as the Pakistan Rickshaw Challenge. Self sustainability.

The guys on this trip, like many of the others, were down-to-earth, humble and hardworking. The volunteers were also incredible, and getting to go deep into rural Bangladesh once more was a delight and environment that I will never get bored of visiting.

Grenfell

In the early hours of June 14th 2017, and during the holy month of Ramadan, I watched online as the horror of a fire in Grenfell Tower, West London took hold. I had come home from Taraweeh prayers and saw it unfold on Sky news, as the flames spread from one side of the tower to engulf the whole thing. It was something that scarred the nation, and is one of the few instances of collective trauma that I have witnessed in the UK. I was working for Penny Appeal at that time, and headed down to the site the following day to assist however I could. I was asked by the then CEO to interview survivors to create an eyewitness film to be given to the impending enquiry. Interviews were being given to news channels, but it just felt wrong for me to be asking for eyewitness accounts in the immediate aftermath. People unaccounted for, posters up everywhere calling for information of those still missing, it was so heavy on the heart, that words just can't sum it up. I remember after the first day, being sat on the tube heading home and breaking down in tears. Then the stories came of those who had been on the phone calling for help, and others who had been with their loved ones as they had tried to flee down poisonous smoke filled stairwells, able to make it out, only to be separated from other family members who didn't. What really struck me was the way not only the community came together but people from around the country came to help. On the flip side of it, the disappointing way that some charities had tried to capitalise on the help they were giving, by promoting the work in the most insensitive way. They shall remain nameless, but those who know, know. I interviewed around ten people who were eyewitnesses and one former resident of the tower itself. Or so he had claimed. It turns out that he was a con artist and fantasist from South London who had claimed he had lost his wife in the tower and was asking for immediate financial help. It seemed odd to me that he was so calm after supposedly losing his wife, and he said he was from Hong Kong, but his name was Vietnamese. Shortly afterwards, he was exposed and ended up in prison. I just don't understand how anyone could try to capitalise on such a tragic and traumatic event. There were others who had lost their homes as the flats around the tower were deemed unsafe, and they had been put into the Westway sport centre for the first few days, then put into temporary accommodation. Many of whom are still there, six years later. According to many campaigners, the London Borough Of Kensington And Chelsea knew that the building was a death trap. Residents had regularly reported blocked stairwells and lack of escape routes, and these calls were ignored. After the fire, it appeared that the Government did little or nothing to help, and even six years later, no one has been brought to justice for knowingly fitting non fire retardant cladding and causing the deaths of at least 72 people, through what was widely considered corporate manslaughter. May their souls rest in peace and those responsible be brought to justice.

*   *   *

In August 2020, I got married to Farah. She is an artist, teacher, curates exhibitions and is a wonderful person. Farah has taken a great interest in my work since we met, and when I was approached by Irfan to take on a challenge to film, I asked Farah if she would join me. K2 is the second highest mountain in the world, set in the Karakoram Mountains in Northern Pakistan. It's the hardest and most dangerous to climb, with less than 500 people summiting and twenty-five percent of those dying on the way back down. In fact, more people have been into space than successfully summited K2 and made it down alive again. We were supposed to do the K2 base camp trek in August 2021, but Covid-19 put a stop to that. Then we both got ill with the Covid-19 Delta variant, where I was hospitalised and was potentially hours from death. I had been coughing up bright red blood, my oxygen saturation had dropped to 84 and I kept hallucinating to the extent where my ensuite bathroom had turned into Westminster Abbey, and there was a knight with a broad sword stood there staring at me. It was when I told Farah this that she called for an ambulance for the second time that week. I thought it might be the angel of death, but then again, I had hypoxia induced visions. After coming through thanks to the amazing Doctors and Nurses of our precious NHS, I started the long road to recovery.

In August 2022 we attempted K2 Basecamp trek with Muslim Charity. Unfortunately, due to a number of factors beyond our control and ill health, our goal wasn't reached, and we had to turn back. However, Farah did run the Pop Art workshop for the children in Hushay valley school as planned, which was immensely successful and hugely inspiring. It was a truly amazing experience for all involved, and we hope that this could be the start of taking the therapeutic value of art to those who truly need it. All funds raised went to supplying water heaters for Hushay Village as the temperature drops to -20C during the winter, and to Muslim Charity's 'Children of the World' campaign, which helps support vulnerable and street children around the world, to get an education and have a safe space to go to.

We will be attempting K2 basecamp once more in 2023 and this time inshaAllah, we will be successful. We are raising funds to build houses for families who lost everything in the floods of in Pakistan in the summer of 2022. There will of course be a full documentary film about this, and another book.

In January 2022 I attended a HEFAT (Hostile Environment and First Aid Training) training course run by a company called Hostile Environment Training, based in Andover. It entails multiple disciplines including; Threat Risk Assessment and Mitigation; Trauma and Emergency Aid; Vehicle Incident First Responder; Electronic Communication; Kidnap and Hostage; Navigation; Vehicle Safety and Security; Landmines, Improvised Explosive Devices and UXO (unexploded ordinance); Conflict Management and Weapon Familiarisation. The course was incredible and I learned so many things that could be helpful in the future, but I hope I never have to use any of them. There was a practical element that I won't go in to, as I don't want to spoil the course, but put it this way, what happened to me was just a mock exercise and had a profound and traumatic effect, so I can't begin to imagine what it would be like in real life. However this is what the course prepares us for, and it really was an amazing experience, with great tuition from a great team that I highly recommend to anyone thinking of going into hostile or remote environments.

*   *   *

I have learned many lessons in the course of being a film maker in the humanitarian sector, and many of these have been retrospectively. It's hard to quantify exactly what I have learned, as some lessons have been so subtle, I may not have noticed them overtly. I know that my film making techniques have evolved; knowing when to film and when to lower the camera; how to communicate and interact with military, security and police personnel in any given situation; what is a necessary story to tell and what feels exploitative; how even after ninety five flights through twenty four countries, checking in to flights at airports still winds me up, and waiting for baggage at the other end annoys me even more; how much mosquitos love feasting on my blood whichever country I am in; how to never ever eat street food if don't want to get sick.

In 2020 I studied and passed an online course at Harvard University titled; Humanitarian Response To Conflict And Disaster. I learned about the complexities of various situations where humanitarian aid is needed. It made me realise that in some situations in the past, I would let emotions take over where pragmatism may have worked better. That acting on feelings and impulse can cause more harm in a volatile or sensitive situation. I have learned to be aware of the safeguarding of children and vulnerable individuals, not just for their own safety in any given environment, but also to respect their privacy and dignity. I am currently studying a UN sponsored course about human rights, and a course on Contemporary Palestinian Realities and Rights. Palestine is a country very close to my heart, and when the worshippers were attacked in Al-Aqsa compound whilst praying during the holy month of Ramadan, something inside me switched, and I couldn't stay silent on the situation. As I have mentioned in chapter 11, I am a humanitarian that strives to adhere to the four humanitarian principles; Humanity, Neutrality, Impartiality and Independence. I also believe that one cannot stay silent when faced with, or observing oppression. This amounts to complicity in my eyes, and ignorance can only be an excuse for so long. When Israel started to bomb Gaza once more and kill innocent men, women and children, I saw nothing on the mainstream news, so I took the initiative to film all of the protests in London and I even filmed and subtitled the main speeches for people to watch and understand what was going on. I will continue to campaign, support and lobby for a free Palestine. I will speak up about injustice and oppression wherever it is in the world. The mainstream media has its own narrative, but with social media and today's multi-platform sharing, the truth as they say, will out.

I have witnessed the horrors, misery and pain of war and of the fallout and effects this can have on a population and the impact it will undoubtedly have for generations to come. I have seen the beauty of the human spirit, of unconditional love. Of genuine care and consideration for fellow humans, adults, elderly and children. I have seen how if you give a man a fish you feed him for a day and if you teach him how to fish, you feed him for a lifetime. And his family. And educate his children. The impact of charity work around the world is often unseen, but is most definitely appreciated by those it helps. My experiences in this field have inspired me to start registering a charity of my own that focuses on Refugees and Internally Displaced People, called Migration Relief. We have already had two deployments in Lebanon and the earthquake zone in Turkey, but these are stories for another time. The longer I spend in this line of work, the more convinced I am that this was the job I was born to do. My faith has deepened and my connection to God and his creations continues to grow on a daily basis. What my journey has shown me in a multitude of situations, is that one small act of kindness to anyone can make a huge difference to their lives. We are all in this together as human kind, which is what I would like to believe we humans intrinsically are; Kind.

I have also faced my innermost fears, and many times brought in to question my motives and agenda. Why do I do this? Am I trying to prove something? What am I trying to prove? To whom am I trying to prove it? In answer to these, I would say that I started doing it for myself. Then it turned into doing it for humanity, and then for the sake of God. I would say that it's a healthy mix of all three today. However, the never ending stream of negative commentary from my own head; the not feeling good enough; the imposter syndrome that plagued me relentlessly; they are still there, but I have learned to ignore them, or at least quieten them down and listen to my heart. And when this doesn't work I just talk to God and ask him to guide me.

My dream of being an adventurer and going to far flung places and doing things most people never get the opportunity to experience, has become a reality. I didn't do these things or visit these places to impress others, although my ego quite enjoys the interest my travel tales can get, therefore I make sure to renew my intentions daily. I did it through a genuine want to do something good, and was prepared to throw my all into whatever came my way. I feel honoured, privileged and thankful to those I have been able to help and am humbled by what I have seen and experienced. There are more missions on the horizon, and in this world where Humanitarian crises are growing by the day, Migration Relief will be doing more work to help those in need. There is also some 'unfinished business' imminent with K2 basecamp part 2!

Did I become Indiana Jones? No. But I did become Matt 'Muhammad Abdul Mateen' Robinson, the Humanitarian Film Maker. I give thanks to God, the most beneficent and most merciful for this opportunity, and pray that I can continue helping to serve humanity. Ameen.

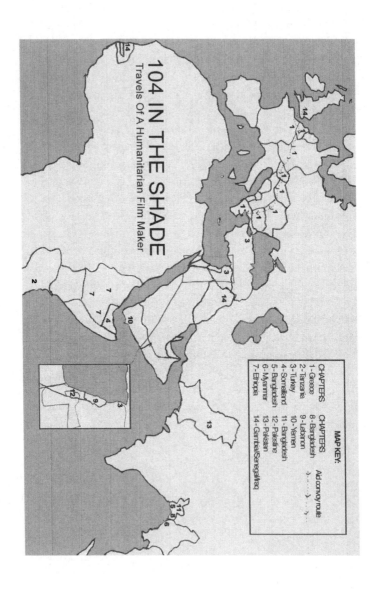

104 IN THE SHADE

Travels Of A Humanitarian Film Maker

MAP KEY:

CHAPTERS
1 - Greece
2 - Tanzania
3 - Turkey
4 - Somaliland
5 - Bangladesh
6 - Myanmar
7 - Ethiopia

CHAPTERS
8 - Bangladesh
9 - Lebanon
10 - Yemen
11 - Bangladesh
12 - Palestine
13 - Pakistan
14 - Gambia/Senegal/Iraq

Aid convoy route
⟶ - ⟶ - ⟶

Me with my mum and dad,
Patricia and Barry Robinson, Summer 1981

My brother Nicholas and I having a snowball fight, Winter 1982

Riding on the front of my Grandfather Alexander
Gifford's tractor, Summer 1983

Yazidi refugee camp, Mount Olympus, Greece

Softex Refugee camp, Thessaloniki, Greece

Muntada Aid and Hope And Aid Direct crew

Sanji Olassiye and his son Oningol
waiting to go in to surgery

The open heart operating theatre, Muhimbili
Hospital, Dar Es Salaam, Tanzania

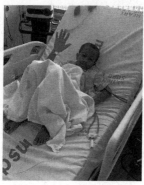

Abdul Razaq in the recovery ward, post operation

New Life Orphanage, set behind the Mosque,
Kirikhan, Turkey

Fatih Mosque, Istanbul, Turkey

A Camel in Burco, Somaliland

Our security escort for the trip, Somaliland

Boys playing football in Netrakona, Bangladesh

The Imam who gave me the name 'Abdul Mateen', and his students

The Bomabardier 400 twin propellor plane. A regular
mode of transport on many of my trips

Rohingya men queue to collect food parcels
in Rakhine state, Myanmar

Buna Coffee beans being freshly roasted in Harar, Ethiopia

Two men having a heated discussion at the
Khat market, Haramaya, Ethiopia

Me feeding a Hyena, Harar, Ethiopia

A view of the highlands, north east of Awassa, Ethiopia

With Irfan Rajput in Ukhia Rohingya refugee camp,
Teknaf, Bangladesh

A Rohingya man carrying Bamboo to construct a hut

Taksima looking out over the vast sprawling Rohingya camp

A memorial to the civil war in Lebanon, which
was fought from 1975 to 1990

The view across the valley,
through razor wire on Mont Liban Castle

An eagle flying over Crater, one of the areas of Aden, Yemen

Yemeni women queueing for water canisters

The beautiful mountains in the desert, outside of Aden

Young stares have seen a thousand lives

A train passing Daulatia brothel, Bangladesh

The orphaned girls we raised money for in
Shaikh Jarrah, Jerusalem, Palestine

The market place in Hebron, where wire mesh was used
to stop Israeli settlers from throwing rocks and other
objects on to Palestinians in the market below

Passing the Palestine flag to Boulos in the final stretch
of the Palestine Half marathon, Bethlehem

The Khatun sisters after Fajr prayer, Dome
Of The Rock, Al Aqsa, Jerusalem

Talking to the Imam of the Dome Of The Rock, with
Muslim Charity's CEO, Maroof Pirzada

Spectators at the horse festival, Layyah, Pakistan

Three of the Punjabi Lancers post event

The rickshaws lined up just before we arrived at
Derawer Fort, Cholistan desert, Pakistan

Senegambia Beach, where the red flags are yellow
and the tides are unforgiving, Gambia

Abdullah, Riz, myself and Faz, somewhere in northern Iraq

Myself, Urfy, Muhammad Ishaq, Farah, Aisha and
Muhammad Ali, Hushay village, northern Pakistan

Farah and I halfway between Hushay village
and Mashabrum basecamp

Printed and bound by CPI Group (UK) Ltd, Croydon, CR0 4YY